THE POCKET GALLERY OF ART

MOTHERS

EVA HOWARTH

GARAMOND

First published in the United Kingdom
by Garamond Ltd, Publishers
Strode House
44-50 Osnaburgh Street
London NW1 3ND

ISBN 1–85583–060–4

Cover design by Tim Scott
Cover paper supplied by
Payhembury Marbled Papers
Payhembury, Devon
Designed by Caroline Reeves
Typeset by J&L Composition Limited
Colour origination by Columbia Offset
Printed in Italy by Rotolito Lombarda

Introduction to

THE POCKET GALLERY OF ART

MOTHERS

The centre of our lives in childhood and a
beloved image forever – 22 artists,
including Correggio, Chardin, Whistler
and Picasso give substance to our ideals of
maternal love and devotion spanning eight
hundred years.

Mercury Instructing Cupid
Correggio (Antonio Allegri)

Italian c.1489–1534   National Gallery, London

The earliest celebrations of motherhood came to us long before Christian belief; ancient Greeks and Romans both worshipped a goddess of Beauty who was also the Mother of Love, and their stories have enlivened Western art ever since. The sixteenth-century preoccupation with pagan mythology was never more delightfully illustrated than in this picture; Cupid is watched with maternal pride by his mother, Venus, as he learns from Mercury.

Although Venus was married to Mars, a jealous husband and the God of War, she also had many lovers and Mercury, the fleet-footed Messenger of the Gods identified by his winged boots, was sometimes named as one of them.

The Renaissance court around Correggio was well-versed in all the classical legends and no doubt appreciated this particular glimpse of a somewhat unconventional 'family'. Such subjects gave artists the excuse for painting nude figures with strong erotic overtones which would otherwise be frowned on by the Church, still the main patron of most great artists.

Correggio took his name from the small Italian town where he was born. Acknowledged as one of the great masters of the Italian High Renaissance, he is known for his altarpieces and ceiling frescoes, but it was his magnificently sensuous painting of mythological subjects that earned him the nickname 'Painter of the Graces'.

The Nativity
Louis Le Nain

French c. 1593–1648   Private Collection

In spite of popular pagan myths, traditional Christian beliefs in the essential purity of motherhood were central to Western Art during the long period of its development.

Medieval artists had usually shown both the Madonna and the Child as symbols but here the light from a torch reveals a very human Child, although the Madonna seems withdrawn into a world of her own, gazing at her child.

Le Nain's simple grouping is set off by the simple red dress, in complete contrast to the elaborate blue gowns of earlier Nativity paintings.

Louis Le Nain was the most talented of three brothers, all of whom were painters. As all three of them signed their paintings only as Le Nain, without any initials, historians have had to decide for themselves on purely stylistic grounds which brother painted which picture; in this serene study, they believe that the shepherds are portraits of all three Le Nains.

Louis is best known for his very realistic paintings of scenes from peasant life, and that is entirely born out by the composition and setting for the Holy Family; his style was a startling innovation in seventeenth-century France.

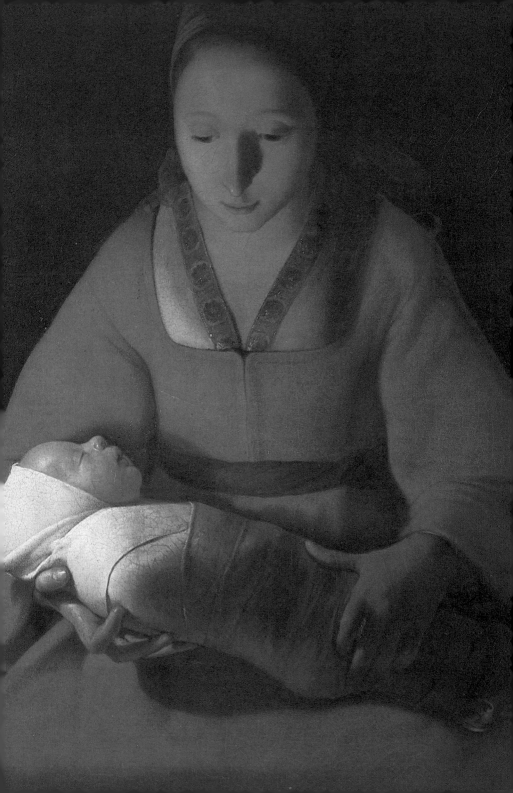

The Newborn Child
Georges de la Tour

French 1593–1652   Musée des Beaux-Arts, Rennes

A young mother sits perfectly still, hardly daring to breathe in case she wakes her newborn child. The stillness, the wonder, the unimaginable joy mixed with fear of the responsibility for another life when her own is only just beginning . . . the scene is apparently so tranquil, and yet so full of emotion that it seems possible that La Tour's models were his own wife and child.

Louis XIII hung one of La Tour's paintings in his bedchamber and was so impressed by it that he soon ordered all the other paintings in the room to be removed. Yet in spite of his royal patron, and considerable success during his life-time, La Tour's work sank into oblivion for almost three hundred years. Today he is regarded as one of the great masters of candlelit scenes.

The recent discovery of the details of his life and of those few of his paintings that survive is an artistic detective story, and even today there are continual arguments over whether his best-known paintings are truly his or contemporary, even modern, fakes. The first chance the public had to see a collection of La Tour's paintings was in Paris in 1972.

Interior with a Woman Peeling Apples
Pieter de Hooch
Dutch 1629–1684   Wallace Collection, London

These interior scenes, one of the glories of Dutch painting, celebrate an entirely new kind of art, with portraits of ordinary people rather than religious symbols or mythical gods. The new, middle-class patrons of the artists wanted their own lives, their homes and their accomplishments on the walls for all to enjoy and admire.

Dutch wives and mothers were respected as down-to-earth, practical members of the household. Here, judging by her modest but elegant clothes, the woman might be the wife of a well-to-do merchant with a number of servants. However, in Holland, a good mother believed firmly in education by example, especially for little girls who were going to be running their own homes one day. It was the pride of every housewife that no matter what time an unexpected visitor might arrive the house would be spotlessly clean and tidy, with plenty of food in the larder for comfortably vast meals and at least one dish of cooked apples on the stove!

De Hooch, an acknowledged master of the use of indoor and outdoor light for special effects, was best-known for his indoor and courtyard scenes. Some were painted to commission, but these interior scenes were also painted on speculation, to catch the eye of a new patron on a visit to the studio. The same fireplace or detail of a bed may turn up in six or seven paintings, presumably modelled on the artist's own home.

Mrs Freake and Baby Mary
Unknown Artist

American c.1670   Worcester Art Museum, Massachusetts

Settlers in the new American colonies were anxious to have their families carefully represented in paintings to adorn the walls of their homes, just as their largely English and Dutch ancestors did. Mrs Freake has obviously put on one of her best dresses, with ribbons and a lace collar, but the American lifestyle is beginning to change some restrictive customs; baby Mary's clothes are far simpler and more practical than her English cousins' would have been. The anonymous artist has not been able to capture very much of a maternal relationship in the faces, but the mother's supporting hand is a lovely touch.

In the villages of New England it was difficult for talented young artists to learn their trade. Some became travelling painters, given commissions by the wealthier settlers, and they were often happy to paint store signs, inn boards, furniture, walls, boxes – in fact anything at all.

The Freake family commissioned a number of paintings in the 1670s and, although the poses are stiff and awkward, the detail is carefully recorded and the painting makes an immediate impression of a vigorous personality.

Saying Grace
Jean-Baptiste-Siméon Chardin
French 1699–1779   Louvre, Paris

The mother is just starting to serve the meal. She stops to help her little son with the next words in the prayer, while his sister seems to be enjoying her brother's difficulties. In the eighteenth century very young boys were dressed in skirts, but the drum hanging on the chair tells us that this is a little boy rather than a girl.

By this time, the Dutch fashion for scenes of everyday middle-class life had spread throughout the rest of Europe, with the mother as the active and central figure of the household. She was now the source of religious education as well as of comfort, food, and nursing care – an image which largely still exists. This scene could have been painted at any time, from seventeenth-century Holland to twentieth-century America, where Norman Rockwell's cover illustrations for *Saturday Evening Post* drew on similar themes.

Chardin was famous for his still-lifes and scenes from bourgeois households. The people in his paintings are, with few exceptions, servant girls, governesses, visitors, bourgeois mothers and children and, occasionally, wealthier women.

The James Family
Arthur Devis
English 1711–1787   Tate Gallery, London

From De Hooch's and Chardin's comfortable middle-class homes to the James's fashionable pretensions; there is no question of mother doing anything mundane like serving dinner or peeling apples; this is a display of wealth and taste rather than family life. Mrs James's gown probably came from Paris, then, as now, the fashion capital of Europe, and her two daughters, one of whom can be seen on the right, are suitably matched in simpler versions, although almost certainly made at home by a local dressmaker from a pattern book. The formal pose, the style of painting that the James chose, and our knowledge of English country life at the time would indicate that the children were brought up by nannies and governesses rather than their mother.

The artist was much concerned, too, that the painting showed off the rich silks and embroidered velvets his clients wore. Hoops – called 'panniers' after the French word for bread basket – were worn to extend skirts sideways; in extreme cases, as much as twelve feet across. It was impossible for two fashionably dressed ladies to sit side by side, let alone hold children on their laps. Even walking through doorways became a problem and curving, open staircases, easy to manoeuvre upon, became popular.

Devis is best-known for his portrait groups, his sitters being mainly rich merchants and country squires who liked to be painted with their families. His pictures tend to be rather formal, with the close attention to costumes seen here a typical feature.

The Countess of Albemarle
George Romney

English 1734–1802   Kenwood House, London

Wealthy women in the eighteenth century had nurses, tutors or governesses to bring up their children, who usually lived on the nursery floor of the house, a long way from the rich and elegant rooms the adults used. When they did meet, usually for an hour or so at tea-time, the children were expected to be on their very best behaviour. They were taught to bow or curtsey to their mother, address her as 'Mama' or 'Madam', and never interrupt her busy life.

Yet, in spite of that, a few mothers and children succeeded in establishing a strong bond of mutual affection and in Romney's portrait the Countess seems to have achieved that sort of relationship with her elder son. There is a glimpse of warmth and mutual regard which makes a pleasant contrast to most society portraits of the time, where the children seem to be used as props in the picture to show off Mama's contribution to the family line.

Romney himself had been brought up in a much less privileged position; in his youth he travelled through the north of England in search of commissions. His usual price was two guineas and by the age of twenty-seven he had managed to save up a hundred pounds, part of which he gave to his wife, departing to London with the remainder.

There he became a successful historical and society portrait painter, best known to the public for his numerous portraits of Lady Hamilton.

Mme Lebrun and Child
Élisabeth Vigée-Lebrun

French 1755–1842   Louvre, Paris

There are surprisingly few artists' paintings of themselves with their children, and because even fewer pre-twentieth-century portrait painters were women, almost none at all where the painter is both mother and subject. So here is a rare example indeed, and the result is delightful in concept, satisfying as a painting, and heart-warming as a subject, showing that a child's affection for its mother can withstand even the most formal bounds of eighteenth-century society.

Élisabeth Vigée-Lebrun started to paint at the age of fifteen. She was still very young when her father died and she supported her mother and herself by making copies of famous paintings, which were eagerly bought by the public. Her work was so admired, and her rise to fame so meteoric, that she was only twenty-seven years old when she painted the first of her many portraits of Queen Marie-Antoinette.

When the French Revolution broke out Mme Vigée-Lebrun left France and travelled extensively throughout Europe, receiving commissions to paint many famous people, among them Lady Hamilton, Madame de Stael, and several members of royalty. After the Revolution she returned to Paris, where her salon became the meeting place of well-known artists.

Yet still her most popular painting is this self-portrait. She was by all accounts a woman of great charm and beauty, which no doubt forms part of its appeal, but the work also conveys a mother's complete enchantment with her daughter, probably the reason for its great success.

The New Dress
John Callcott Horsley
English 1817–1903   Private Collection

The little girl is clearly delighted with her new silk dress and the scene is made even more enjoyable by the attentive dog gazing adoringly at his small companion. The far-away look on her mother's face might be caused by the cost of the soon-to-be outgrown outfit, complete with velvet satin-lined coat.

The Victorian revival of Dutch family scenes was probably encouraged by the matriarchal influence of the English Queen, and her insistence that children should be an integral part of everyday life, whether in her own palace or in a simpler country home, like the one represented here. One small anachronism gives the painter away – in an original seventeenth-century Dutch painting, the oriental rug would probably have been on the table, rather than on the floor.

Horsley first made his name as a painter of historical subjects; he was also a musician, a friend of Mendelssohn and a regular contributor of drawings to Punch. Later he began to specialize in contemporary scenes variously described as 'sunshine and pretty women' and 'flirtation in the countryside'.

It was all very decorously done. Indeed, when he became Rector of the Royal Academy in his late fifties, he caused some trouble by his objections to nude models. As a result he became popularly known as Clothes-Horsley.

In the Park
Berthe Morisot

French 1841–1895   Museum de Petit Palais, Paris

Madame Morisot was a very attractive woman whose paintings reflect much of her own charm and femininity. Many of her paintings show one of her favourite models, her own daughter Julie, whose life she recorded from the cradle to young womanhood. Frequently there are two children in the picture; the second girl is usually Jeannie Gobillard, her niece and Julie's playmate.

Berthe Morisot came from a well-to-do family; her father was a patron of the arts and encouraged his daughter in her ambition to be a painter. She was fortunate in becoming the pupil and life-long friend of Edouard Manet, whose brother she eventually married.

The park in the picture is probably the Bois-de-Boulogne in Paris, not very far from the artist's studio. As a member of the Impressionist circle her paintings were regularly exhibited at the Paris Salon and at other venues, but her reputation grew posthumously until today her paintings are highly regarded as a true reflection of her time.

The Artist's Mother
James Abbott McNeill Whistler
American 1834–1903   Louvre, Paris

To the general public this is probably one of the most famous pictures of all, and certainly the one that springs to mind immediately on the subject of artists and motherhood. It is a long way from the pastel happiness of Impressionist children with their pretty mothers; it has beauty rather than prettiness, with an atmosphere of serenity, dignity, and a certain withdrawal from emotional ties; this is a record of a life coming to a close.

This portrait of Mrs George Washington Whistler, known always as Whistler's Mother, is signed with a butterfly, his usual signature. The painting was bought by the city of Paris in 1891.

James McNeill Whistler was born in the United States, but during part of his boyhood he lived at the Russian Court, where his father was working for the Tsar. After a number of years studying in Paris he came to England, where he spent most of his working life.

He became a very successful painter but was not personally the most popular of men; he once lost all his money when he brought an action for libel against an offensive art critic.

The Bellelli Family
Edgar Degas

French 1834–1917   Louvre, Paris

The mother of the two little girls is the Baroness Bellelli, Degas's aunt. The severity of the striking black and white composition is softened by the patterned carpet, wallpaper and, most clearly, the picture on the wall. One feels that Degas was more interested in the composition than the sitters; perhaps at the time two little girls weren't as exciting a project as the ballet dancers or circus performers which he admired and painted so often.

Strangely enough, unlike other Impressionists, Edgar Degas never painted from nature. He would work from notes, sketches and a large number of drawings, but would always paint the final picture in his studio.

Degas hated to part with his paintings. After his death four important sales were held in Paris to dispose of the hundreds of works which were found in his studio.

Gabrielle and her Children
Pierre-Auguste Renoir

French 1841–1919   Musée d'Orsay, Paris

There is no doubt that Renoir loved painting the female sex from small, wide-eyed babies to richly sensual women at moments of quiet intimacy, in the bath, sitting in the garden, playing with their children. Gabrielle, a simple peasant girl with the sturdy body and round face that Renoir adored, lived originally as a servant with Madame and Monsieur Renoir and their three children, but she also became Renoir's model and had children by him. Their extended family was celebrated by the artist in many portraits and drawings, and the deep affection he felt for them shows clearly in the rounded composition, the warm colours and the physical closeness of the three bodies in this painting.

By this time the work of the Impressionists had begun to make art critics and the general public revise their earlier opinions. In their early days nearly all the group had had a hard struggle and few dealers were willing to buy their work. Paintings which today sell for a fortune sold originally for the price of a canvas or a dinner – but gradually Impressionism became admired and Renoir was among those who became famous and successful.

Orana Maria
Paul Gauguin

French 1848–1903   Metropolitan Museum of Art, New York

The Tahitian title of the painting can be translated as 'We Greet Thee, Mary'. Gauguin shows Mary and the Child as he thought the islanders would visualize them, choosing for his models a Tahitian woman and her son, dressed in native fashion. In the background flowering trees form a typical local scene. The painting conveys too the easy-going and fundamentally happy life of Tahitian women. Naturally enough, this was seen as appalling blasphemy by the conventional Christian world, and Gauguin's reputation suffered from the resentment and even hysteria that his work inspired in Europe, where depicting the Madonna as a native woman was seen as degrading the reverence shown to her.

Paul Gauguin was a successful stockbroker before he became a painter. At the age of forty-three he decided to turn his back on civilization and went to live on the idyllic island of Tahiti. In his book Noa Noa, he wrote: 'I have escaped everything that is artificial and conventional. Here I enter into truth, become one with nature'. In spite of poverty and continual illness he painted his greatest pictures during this period.

Sleeping Mother
Christian Krohg

Norwegian 1852–1925   Private Collection

The mother is clearly exhausted by the day spent with a demanding child, and she is painted sleeping profoundly alongside her baby. This is a tender study of a moment which must strike a chord of sympathy in most mothers struggling to bring up their children in a simple household. There is quiet reality in every corner of the room, not the immaculate household of the Dutch sixteenth century, but a modern nursery, with its brightly-painted, comfortable, even shabby furniture.

Christian Krohg specialized in depicting domestic and country scenes, and this is his most popular painting.

The theme of mother and child is a common one in art, from the religious adoration of medieval Madonnas to the gentle humanity of this century. Yet it was not until the twentieth century that in America a special day in the year was chosen for honouring 'motherhood' – a time to say thank you to the unsung heroines of the nursery. The idea was put forward by Anna Jarvis, who lived in Philadelphia, in 1907. Four years later Mother's Day was celebrated in every state, and the custom has now spread to other countries in Europe, Latin America, Africa and even in the Far East.

The Lunch
Claude Monet

French 1840–1926   Frankfurt Kunstinstitut, Frankfurt

The scene is a typical French middle-class dining room. The maid has set the table, and mother and son are sitting waiting for father to appear. His napkin is neatly folded and so is his newspaper. The wine is placed next to his glass. In short, everything is ready for father to enjoy his lunch; here is a painting which shows clearly that even at the beginning of the century, the world of women and children was incomplete until the centre of the household – and the only figure missing from the painting – appeared. Yet it was all done with affection and with supremely French style; the more so since it is possible that this was Monet's own family.

The word 'Impressionism' originated from a painting of Claude Monet's, called *Impression, Rising Sun*, which was first exhibited in 1874. An art critic coined the word with the intention of ridiculing the group of artists who painted in the new style.

Monet's work consisted largely of landscapes and a few still-lifes which showed a masterly presentation of atmosphere and colour. However, at the beginning of his career art dealers were still reluctant to buy from him and so he painted more conventional pictures, such as *The Lunch*, which he hoped would amuse and attract the general public.

Mother and Child
Bernard de Hoogh
Dutch 1867–1943   Private Collection

The girl in the picture no doubt sees the doll as her own child with whom she must act the mother, as little girls have done through the ages. Baby dolls have been known since the earliest civilizations, and in many cultures dolls symbolize childhood itself – in Japan women wanting children have offered them at shrines, while child brides in India have commonly been presented with them.

The making of dolls and doll's houses has been a considerable industry in Europe for some three centuries. The products have become more and more sophisticated, and the modern child can buy for her doll a wonderful range of furniture, clothes and household equipment in miniature.

The finest dolls and doll's houses can be seen in museums. These are not just playthings but works of art in their own right, perfect miniatures which arouse delight and amazement at the way they reflect each century's fashions and customs.

Some of the finest dolls of all have been, and continue to be, produced in the Netherlands. Little is known about de Hoogh, a modern inheritor of the traditional Dutch fascination with household scenes, but he knew enough about children to give the girl's doll the importance it deserved.

Luxembourg Gardens
Pierre de Belay
French 1890–1947   Musée des Beaux-Arts, Rouen

In every big city there are certain parks which attract mothers with young children. The Luxembourg Gardens, on the left bank of Paris, is one of these. There is even a puppet show there every afternoon and for older children there are statues representing all the queens of France as well as a group of figures of outstanding women from the nineteenth century.

Little is known about Pierre de Belay, but he was obviously influenced by the bright colours and simple shapes of the 1920s. The girls' clothes are smart and cheerful without being fussy, making areas of bright colour and giving an impression of a warm, sunny day in spring. These are comparatively modern mothers, taking care of their own children, enjoying time out for a little gossip and a drink of lemonade before going back to do the housework.

The history of the park goes back to the seventeenth century when Maria de' Medici, widow of Henry IV of France, built the Luxembourg Palace. The extensive green area around it, with its shady trees and wide gravel walks, was the meeting place of fashionable society. Today the palace is the seat of the Senate and the park is still a popular meeting place for university students, foreign visitors and, of course, mothers, who come from all over the city to spend the afternoon with their friends and their children.

Mother and Child
Pablo Picasso

Spanish 1881–1973   Private Collection

Picasso is probably the best-known and certainly the most versatile artist of the twentieth century. During his long career he experimented with various new techniques and painted in a number of different styles.

Mother and Child was painted during his so-called 'blue period', which lasted from approximately 1901 to 1905. During most of this period Picasso was himself very poor and his paintings reflect a great understanding of, and compassion towards, human suffering, a subject to which he frequently returned in later life.

The woman in the painting could be any mother trying to remove her child from some disaster – war, famine or other calamity. The solitary figure standing against a vast sea conveys a tremendous sense of loneliness and despair.

The sombre mood of Picasso's paintings of this period is emphasized by the cold greenish-blue colour which dominates most of them. However, a sense of hope is conveyed by the single red flower in the mother's hand.

Market Scene
L. S. Lowry

English 1887–1976   Salford Museum, Salford

In *Market Scene* mothers with their children are seen queueing, choosing, bargaining. In 1939, when this picture was painted, unemployment was high, especially in industrial cities, and women with large families often had a hard time making ends meet.

Lowry painted this world all his life, involving himself vicariously in the life of the town, with the people he saw on the street, creating little stories so you can see exactly who they are, where they are going, and even perhaps what they are going to do next! His colours are mainly subdued, and most of his pictures look as if they were seen through a thin layer of smog. But the figures are full of humour and individual character and gain emphasis from the plain white background, a characteristic feature of many of this artist's paintings.

Lowry lived most of his life in an industrial suburb of Manchester. He was in his early twenties when his family, because of financial problems, first moved there. His mother hated the place so much that for the next seven years until her death she refused to leave the house. Lowry, on the other hand, became fascinated by his environment. In his job as rent collector he could observe and record, although he always regarded his paintings as private scribbles, and it took a long time before his growing reputation as an artist made him famous.

Ironing Day
Ditz (Dietlinde Nekuda)
Austrian living artist   Private Collection

The woman here is Ditz herself and the little girl is her daughter. This is another rare example of a female artist painting a self-portrait with child, but it is a very far cry from Madame Vigée-Lebrun's romantic image; this is modern reality. The setting is a spare room in the painter's house which is used for ironing, sewing and any other household chores.

The little girl is surrounded by books. It was an established custom in the family that whenever the artist had to do the ironing or sewing her daughter would come and read aloud to her.

On the floor, next to her toys and books, is a diabolo, an ancient children's game; on the wall is a picture of roses painted on glass with a corn dolly hanging beneath it, both of which are popular art forms in Austria. So the painting is a record of family history as well as a charming genre scene of modern life.

Dietlinde Nekuda was born in Vienna, married an Englishman and now lives in London. She signs all her paintings 'Ditz', an abbreviation of Dietlinde. *Ironing Day* was exhibited in the Royal Academy, London, in 1987.

Sources

CORREGGIO: *Mercury Instructing Cupid*
National Gallery, London

LE NAIN: *The Nativity*
Private Collection (Bridgeman)

DE LA TOUR: *The Newborn Child*
Musée des Beaux-Arts, Rennes (Bridgeman)

DE HOOCH: *Interior with a Woman Peeling Apples*
Wallace Collection, London

ANON: *Mrs Freake and Baby Mary*
Worcester Art Museum, Massachusetts

CHARDIN: *Saying Grace*
Louvre, Paris (Bridgeman)

DEVIS: *The James Family*
Tate Gallery, London

ROMNEY: *The Countess of Albemarle*
Kenwood House, London

LE BRUN: *Mme Le Brun and Child*
Louvre, Paris (Bridgeman)

HORSLEY: *The New Dress*
Private Collection (Bridgeman)

MORISOT: *In the Park*
Musée du Petit Palais, Paris (Bridgeman)

WHISTLER: *The Artist's Mother*
Louvre, Paris (Bridgeman)

DEGAS: *The Bellelli Family*
Louvre, Paris (Bridgeman)

RENOIR: *Gabrielle and her Children*
Musée d'Orsay, Paris (Bridgeman)

GAUGUIN: *Orana Maria*
Metropolitan Museum, New York

KROHG: *Sleeping Mother*
Billedgalleri, Bergen

MONET: *The Lunch*
Stüdelschische Kunstinstitut, Frankfurt

DE HOOGH: *Mother and Child*
Galerie George, London (Bridgeman)

DE BELAY: *Luxembourg Gardens*
Musée des Beaux-Arts, Rouen (Bridgeman)

PICASSO: *Mother and Child*
Christie's, London (Bridgeman)

LOWRY: *Market Scene*
Salford Art Gallery and Museum (Bridgeman)

DITZ: *Ironing Day*
Private Collection (Bridgeman)

BY LAWRENCE GOWING

THE MUSEUM OF MODERN ART, NEW YORK

Distributed by Doubleday & Company, Garden City, New York

henri
matisse
64
paintings

© The Museum of Modern Art, 1966
11 West 53 Street, New York, N. Y. 10019

Library of Congress Catalogue Card Number 66-26205
Designed by Joseph Bourke Del Valle
Printed in the U. S. A.

This book records the fourth exhibition of the paintings of Henri Matisse held at The Museum of Modern Art. The first, directed by Alfred H. Barr, Jr., was in 1931, the Museum's second year. In 1951, upon the occasion of the large retrospective also directed by Mr. Barr, the Museum published his monumental volume, *Matisse: His Art and His Public*. It was definitive as of that date, when Matisse still had three prolific years before him. The great cut gouaches of Matisse's last phase were shown separately in 1961.

The present exhibition has a twofold purpose: first, to bring to a younger generation the work of one of the supreme masters of our century, who pioneered in so many areas and laid the foundations for various modern movements; and second, to show for the first time in New York a number of significant examples from the artist's estate, which epitomize his development at different periods throughout his life.

On behalf of the Trustees of The Museum of Modern Art, I wish to thank His Excellency, The French Ambassador, Charles Lucet, for his gracious sponsorship of the exhibition, and Mr. Edouard Morot-Sir, Cultural Counselor of the French Embassy, for his kind assistance in facilitating the loans from France. We are especially indebted to the artist's daughter, Madame Georges Duthuit, and to his sons, Messrs. Jean and Pierre Matisse, for their generous and courteous cooperation. We are grateful to them and to all the other lenders listed on page 61, without whose sympathetic interest and generosity the exhibition would not have been possible.

My special thanks go to Mr. Lawrence Gowing, Keeper of British Painting at The Tate Gallery, London, for his brief narration of Matisse's heroic career and his perceptive analysis of the master's innovations, particularly as they underlie and prophesy subsequent tendencies in art both in Europe and America.

In preparing the exhibition and this book, I have been guided at every point by Mr. Barr's deep understanding of Matisse's work. I wish also to acknowledge the help extended by Mrs. Sidney F. Brody, Mr. Bernard Dorival, Mr. Frank Perls, Mr. Perry T. Rathbone, Mr. John Rewald, and Mr. Frederick S. Wight.

I have particularly benefited by consulting the excellent catalogue of the large Matisse retrospective, organized by the University of California at Los Angeles and subsequently shown at The Art Institute of Chicago and the Museum of Fine Arts in Boston; the interested student is referred to that catalogue, which antedates this volume by only a few months.

Miss Alicia Legg, Associate Curator of Painting and Sculpture Exhibitions, has been my loyal coadjutor throughout, and has also installed the exhibition. Other colleagues at the Museum whom I wish to thank for devoted assistance of various kinds are Miss Frances Keech, Mrs. Jennifer Licht, Miss Sarah Elliston, Miss Françoise Boas, Mrs. Cicely Speicher, Miss Helen M. Franc, and Mr. Joseph Bourke Del Valle.

Monroe Wheeler
Director of the Exhibition

Some painters seek out art as if by instinct and fall on it with fury; some of them receive it at birth and enter the inheritance with a kind of scorn. Matisse, by contrast, came to painting late and seriously. He accepted the styles of the nineteenth century, as he came to know them, without apparent reservations, and some of their essence remained with him always. In 1895, at the age of twenty-five, he was a capable student in a conventional (but none-theless sensitive) academic style, which continued as if Manet had never lived. He was on the verge of a respectable success, with no disposition to overturn anything.

He was hardly aware of the existence of impressionism until he was twenty-seven. Then he discovered it as well as some of the developments that had already succeeded it. Even so, he showed no particular facility. Gustave Moreau, his teacher, commended Toulouse-Lautrec, but all that Matisse learned at the Moulin de la Galette was the tune of the Farandole—he found himself whistling it thirty-five years later while he painted Dr. Barnes's mural. It was the style of modern painting—the color and the touch—rather than its view of life that affected him.

The *Dinner Table*, 1897 (p. 22), which he painted for exhibition at Moreau's suggestion, looks now like an unexceptional impres-sionist picture. It is distinguished by a clear iridescence of color, but there is also a certain moderation, which avoids disrupting the real solidity of things. The *Dinner Table* was nonetheless objectionable to Matisse's academic supporters, and in the pictures that followed his response was altogether more personal and extreme. The pure colors of impressionism, as he wrote later in a statement that has a good deal of autobiography in it, "proved to the next generation that these colors . . . contain within them, independent of the ob-jects that they serve to represent, the power to affect the feel-ings. . . ." [23]

Matisse's feelings were evidently and unexpectedly involved. The brightness of impressionist color stimulated, in the next few years, a series of pictures that were increasingly impetuous and free. *Side-board and Table*, 1899 (p. 22), reflects the divisionist manner of the neo-impressionists, but with none of their methodical system. The color is pursued for its own sake; it slides easily into arbitrary and enchanting lilac and turquoise. The application of the paint has evidently a fascination of its own; a spot is apt to land delicately in the middle of the touch before, gaining from it a complementary

Superior numbers in the text refer to books in the alphabetical list of references on page 55.

nimbus. Other pictures are less precise. Some of them are freely dappled with color, rather in the manner of Bonnard. The two men were moving in opposite directions: the way in which Matisse set green against orange or scarlet against violet was in comparison strangely impulsive, almost reckless. Painting from the window of his apartment on the Quai St. Michel, he made an impatient cascade of pink and green brushstrokes spell evening light on the towers of Notre Dame. Other pictures that he was painting at thirty, among them the *Male Model*, c. 1900 (p. 23), adopted the most forceful of the post-impressionist ways with color. Yet the aspect of Cézanne they followed was not so much the basic analysis as the boldness, the quality of pictorial statement.

In style these pictures are various and discrepant, but they have in common a continual and deliberate audacity with color. They give the first glimpse of an element in Matisse's artistic constitution that reappears at the crucial points of his development. Though nothing in his art is uncalculated, the precipitate mood of these pictures already had more of the boldness of modern painting, more of its compulsive response, regardless of consequences, to require-ments inherent in the picture, than almost anything in the art of the 1890's. Late in his life he described the frame of mind in which the impetus came to him: "Although I knew I had found my true path . . . I took fright, realizing that I could not turn back. So I charged head down . . . urged forward by I knew not what—a force that I see today is quite alien to my normal life as a man." [14]

Nevertheless Matisse's beginning left him with a sense that the chromatic substance of painting was real and credible, a sense that his juniors hardly shared. He never adopted the ironic detachment with which Picasso, for example, took up the styles of the 1890's. Pure color seems to have held for him a special value that debarred him from the kind of facility that was in the air. The prodigality of Derain and Vlaminck, his colleagues in the next few years, and the airy lightness of Braque's manner under their influence were both equally foreign to him. Matisse and Derain had studied together in 1899; two years later Derain introduced Matisse to Vlaminck, with whom he was working at Chatou. But while the younger men con-tinued from the point Matisse had reached, Matisse himself hesi-tated. The hardship of his personal life with no patron or dealer to support him was a deterrent; by nature he was a prey to obsessional anxiety, and he had good reason for it now. He was married, with three children; in 1900 he was painting exhibition decorations by the yard at the Grand Palais for a living, and during the following years he was often unable to keep his family together.

Moreover, he regarded his apprenticeship as still unfinished.

Matisse studied everything, always, and never without enormous labor; he worked from morning to dusk all his life to ensure that the apparent spontaneity of art should be thoroughly rehearsed. In 1900 he was rehearsing self-identification with the expression of an animal-like passion. He would hurry from his hack work to night school to model a jaguar after Barye. The study itself was obsessionally rigorous. He devoted months to it and before he could finish it he had to borrow a dissected cat from a medical student to examine the articulation of the spine and the tail. He explained that his object was "to identify himself with the passion of the beast, expressed in the rhythm of the volumes."[15] He was evidently confident that the passion could be studied as objectively, and by the same methods, as other constituents of art had traditionally been studied. At first consideration the idea seems incongruous, yet it is characteristic. The animal quality, the natural force of impulse, had a special value to him, and he cultivated it. The nickname les fauves, the wild beasts, which his circle was given five years later when the full force of his originality burst on the public, was welcome to him.

For the time being Matisse's paintings were far from ferocious. Paintings like Carmelina, 1903 (p. 24), were relatively somber, rigorously studied from life and modeled in deep tone. Their force was wholly traditional. Technically, Matisse was consolidating his ground, but he was also pondering the implications of his earlier audacity. Unlike Vlaminck, who thought visiting the Louvre sapped one's strength, Matisse was well aware of what tonal modeling had to offer, and of the whole tradition of pictorial structure that went with it. Matisse possessed, as the counterpart of his recurrent boldness, an almost equally persistent streak of caution. It was a part of his strength; he never moved until the way ahead was clear. All his life his development proceeded by alternate forward steps and pauses. When the time came for each step he was entirely convinced of its rightness and beauty, and ready to hold forth on the subject—almost too ready for some of his friends.

The special significance of Cézanne for Matisse was that he had sacrificed neither color nor structure, and when Matisse went to the South in 1904 he still had Cézanne in mind; Cézanne was always an example of moral resolution to him, a talisman. But Signac, established nearby at St. Tropez, provided a more immediate and dominating influence. Neo-impressionism was the fashion, and a deliberate, methodical system had a special virtue to "the anxious, the madly anxious Matisse," as Cross, who lived a little distance away and watched the process of conversion, described him. The unbridled force of color had run away with him once: the controlled neo-impressionist style was welcome. Moreover the wide-spaced lozenges of paint isolated elemental ingredients of painting—the effect of one pure color on another and the energy that is inherent in a brushstroke.

Matisse, as he said, "never avoided the influence of other artists. I should have thought it a form of cowardice and a lack of sincerity toward myself."[1] Yet the style of Signac and Cross became in his hands a curiously personal one. The sophisticated manner was followed as if naively for its own sake, so that the last traces of impressionistic illusion dissolved and only the bare visual elements were left. His neo-impressionist sketches, despite the busy brushstrokes, have a suggestion already of his later simplifications. In style the picture that he made out of them, with its complementary haloes, followed Signac and Cross; in composition it had affinities with symbolism and the bathers of Cézanne (see study for Luxe, Calme et Volupté, 1904, p. 25). But it also contained something of Matisse's own that was independent of all of them. The couplet from Baudelaire's L'Invitation au voyage, from which he took his title, was like a motto:

> Là, tout n'est qu'ordre et beauté
> Luxe, calme et volupté.

Matisse had discovered within the post-impressionist apparatus, which had been devised to deal directly with the world, the possibility of quite a different and opposite purpose. The pictorial means, with their richness and profusion, could hold a quality of tranquility that offered an escape from all that oppressed him.

Signac was delighted with Luxe, Calme et Volupté, and bought it, but the Indian summer of neo-impressionism was over. It had served its purpose for Matisse; the intrinsic qualities that he found in it were of more significance than the means by which he reached them. In the works that followed, the orderliness was by no means so apparent and the neo-impressionist system was progressively transformed.

The stimulus of pure color provoked another headlong rush, apparently as impetuous as the first. The pictures exhibited in the fall of 1905, which earned Matisse and his friends the name of wild beasts, had the appearance of arbitrary fury both in the color and in the brush that applied it. But Matisse's color was now directed by a very positive purpose. Turning away from the full spectrum of neo-impressionism, he reduced his palette until it was dominated by the fiercest oppositions in it. His new pictures revolved round the poles of red and green. The harsh polarity in itself set them apart from the characteristic schemes of all the painting under the sign of impressionism, schemes that were aligned with the poles of yellow

and violet or orange and blue, the oppositions that carry the illusion of light and shadow and the implication of atmosphere and space. The combination of red and green offers precisely the reverse. It denies depth; it insists on the painted surface. The pictures of the latter part of 1905 were above all pictures of red and green, reflecting the elation of his escape from the naturalistic spectrum.

The light in these pictures is of another kind. Where red and green meet something happens; there is a continuous, fluorescent palpitation as between no other colors. It may be that the eye detects the possibility, even the minute consummation, of the additive mixture that forms yellow, an effect more real and more surprising than anything in neo-impressionist theory. At all events, the extremity of the contrast in hue between equivalent tones sets up a dazzling vibration. It is such vibrations that give light to pictures like the *Open Window*, 1905 (p. 8). The brush responds with animation to the drama of the conjunction. The colors of fauvism meet as equals; only their functions differ. Sometimes an intense red line is balanced against inert green masses. In a picture of Madame Matisse called *Woman with Hat*, 1905 (p. 13), it is the green that passes around and between the patches of scarlet, orange, and violet that denote the model, as if exploring the medium of existence in which the colors float together, and exploring also a human quality—probing the meaning of the elegance and discovering a moroseness in the modish pose. Combining red with green and adding to them an intense dark blue, Matisse began to deal with the intrinsic properties of color. The whole of his subsequent practice was, in a sense, an extension of the discovery of 1905. When he came to teach, he distinguished two methods—"one considering color as warm and cool" in the impressionist manner, "the other seeking light through the opposition of colors."[2] The latter was Matisse's way, and he pursued it almost without interruption for the rest of his life, placing color against color and revealing an inherent light in the interval and the interplay between them.

There is little in the preceding pictures to prepare one for the style of 1905. The examples of both Signac and Cézanne certainly pointed toward painting made solely out of color, and recollections of Gauguin may have done more than either to suggest the combination of red and green. But the precedent that Matisse studied most closely and the one that fortified him best was undoubtedly his own. "I found myself, or my artistic personality," he told Apollinaire, "by considering my early works. I discovered in them something constant which I took at first for monotonous repetition. It was the sign of my personality, which came out the same no matter what different moods I had passed through."[24] The self-regarding habit, indeed the engrossment in himself, that the words betray was characteristic; it was a vital part of his equipment. It led him to a frank acceptance of the painter as the single significant source of his painting, and the recognition that the painting records more about him than he knows himself. Matisse, who was almost oblivious of how he appeared to others, gave some of the first and clearest descriptions of the reflexive realism of modern art.

It was the pictures of five years and more earlier that gave the clue to the way ahead in 1905. They taught him not only boldness, but also a confidence that the kind of painting that was natural to him was based on oppositions of pure color. But paintings like the *Open Window* had, again, an agitated brilliance. They belied the *calme* that was essential to him. Moreover, painting that was based on oppositions of color needed to be planned in clearly mapped-out areas on the picture surface. In the next portrait of his wife the green was fixed and identified as a stripe of shadow between the pinkness of light and the ochre reflection. The accents of red and green in *Reading* were still scattered rapturously across the canvas. But when he turned again to the mood of arcadian felicity, which epitomized what he most needed from art, the impulsive spontaneity was replaced by a deliberation of design that was new to him.

Joy of Life. (1905-06). Oil on canvas, 68½ x 93¾". The Barnes Foundation, Merion, Pennsylvania (Not in Exhibition)

Open Window. (1905). Oil on canvas, 21¾ x 18⅛". Collection Mr. and Mrs. John Hay Whitney, New York

9

To look at *Joy of Life*, 1905-06 (p. 9), one must go to the Barnes Foundation in Merion, Pennsylvania, yet one bears it in mind as an imaginary part of any Matisse exhibition. It was the turning point in a struggle that continued nearly all his life, swaying first one way then the other, the struggle (as he wrote long after) with the viewpoint "current at the time I first began to paint, when it was permissible only to render observations made from nature."[23] It was a struggle with a part of himself. The shortcomings of impressionism had been the subject of avant-garde discussion for twenty years, but Matisse's critical attitude toward it took a special personal turn. The properties of light and color were more precious to him than to any other painter, yet he had a peculiar awareness of the dangers that beset them. There was an ever-present threat that the effect would prove transitory. The attempt "to register fleeting impressions" was obviously vulnerable, but Matisse's training had left him with a conviction that the process of conception must pass through "a certain analytical phase." The opposite method, the intellectual synthesis, held exactly the same danger. "When the synthesis is immediate, it is premature, without substance, and the impoverished expression comes to an insignificant conclusion, ephemeral and momentary."[9]

Matisse's whole development was a search for the kind of light that could be depended on to last—and the preoccupation gave Cézanne a special significance to him. He understood Cézanne earlier and better than any of his contemporaries, but his own standpoint was different and he had a talent for distinguishing between an example and a pattern. His attention was concentrated not only on achieving something durable like the art of the museums, but even more on the attainment of a continuous, undisturbed condition—as if the primary object were an inward bliss, which almost anything outside himself might interrupt. He had an obsessive concern with continuity in itself. "One can judge of the vitality and power of an artist when . . . he is able to organize his sensations to return in the same mood in different days."[17] Light changes, and with it one's impressions; obviously art could not depend on them. Yet for Matisse, in one sense or another, it always did depend on them. He needed light to see the picture and one kind of impression was indispensable, his impressions of his own painting. Eventually he discovered the answer, sitting quite still in an apartment in Nice. In old age, when a radio interviewer asked why the Midi held him, he answered: "Because in order to paint my pictures I need to stay for a number of days under the same impressions. . . ."[6]

Divisionism and fauvism were both inherited from the empirical outlook of the nineteenth century, and both depended on transitory sensations and the evanescent brushmark. The very immediacy of the effect was disturbing, "I want," he wrote, "to reach that condensation of sensations that constitutes a picture."[17] For him, painting existed apart in a region of ideal detachment. The great picture at Merion portrayed it.

The sensations that were condensed in *Joy of Life* were at root experiences of art. The title forms another of Matisse's revealing mottoes, and an appropriate one: he looked to art for the undisturbed ideal bliss of living. All the material of the picture—the conventional arcadia, the juxtapositions of color, which were developed from his sketches, and the accented contour—came in one way or another out of other paintings. The rhythmic drawing was a new development; Matisse once remarked that he preferred Ingres's *Odalisque* to Manet's *Olympia* because "the sensual and willfully determined line of Ingres seemed to conform better to the needs of painting."[24] Ingres's *Bain turc* had been shown at the Salon d'Automne the year before, but the influence, like everything else in *Joy of Life*, was transformed. The consistency of the picture was indeed willfully determined; it reflected a new idea of the needs of painting.

In the foreground of *Joy of Life* rose-pink lovers lie against deep blue-grey and purple grass. Beyond them the same combination of pink and blue outlines the reclining women in a long arabesque. In the distance, dusky pink melts out of the sky across the blue-grey sea. The radiance is concentrated in the center of the lemon-yellow ground. Under the trees it turns into scarlet and orange; emerald green curls through them, making the stem of a tree on one side, foliage on the other. Each color is sinuously outlined, not against its complementary but rather against an amicable counterpart, in a refined and consistent color system of Matisse's own. There is an air of resplendent artifice and a delicate yet extravagant disproportion. "Observations made from nature" are forgotten.

The new condition of painting was quiet and detached; it was *cool*, in a way that empirical and impulsive painting could never be. It was devised deliberately, with much labor. Discussing the picture Matisse explained why: "I painted it in plain flat colors because I wanted to base the quality of the picture on a harmony of all the colors in their plainness. I tried to replace the vibrato with a more expressive, more direct harmony, simple and frank enough to provide me with a restful surface."[16]

The early fauve style, like the paintings of five years before, had been found wanting in the quality that Matisse most needed from art: *calme*. "There was a time," he wrote later, and he may have been thinking of the turn of the century or of 1905, "when I never left my paintings hanging on the wall, because they reminded me of moments of nervous excitement, and I did not care to see them again when I was quiet." [17] The need for harmonious quietness preoccupied him continually. When he began to paint, as he remembered in old age, what meant most to him was that "then I was free, solitary, and quiet." [25]

Matisse once explained his tendency to simplify: "It is only that I tend toward what I feel; toward a kind of ecstasy . . . and then I find tranquility."[26] It may be that all painting is intended, among other things, to present some ideal state. But the quietness that Matisse sought—the plainness of pure color and the "restful surface"—had, evidently, a special significance to him. His ideal not only excluded what was momentary or potentially transitory; it avoided equally anything that was disturbingly expressive. The idea of expression itself had to be redefined until, as he eventually told Georges Duthuit, it was "one and the same thing as decoration." Anything disquieting was unwelcome. Behind the attitude to art there was an acute intolerance of whatever was in any way disturbing or oppressive, and not in art only. He sought in art, and in life as well, hermetic conditions of private self-preservation. When he tried with his usual candor to describe them, he arrived at a definition that seems at first sight extraordinarily inert and self-protective:

> What I dream of is an art of balance, of purity and serenity devoid of troubling or disturbing subject matter . . . like a comforting influence, a mental balm—something like a good armchair in which one rests from physical fatigue.[17]

It is not unusual to require from art a solace and a refuge. Matisse was unique in the realism with which he recognized the need; the resourcefulness with which he pursued it amounted to genius. He demanded of art the expression of an ideal state of being. He did not merely require a representation of a perfect world, although he sought that as well in several different forms. His object was not even directly sensuous. The senses were continuously engaged, but Matisse half-mistrusted them: sensual gratification was itself precarious. Looking at Titian and Veronese, "those wrongly termed Renaissance masters . . . I found in them superb fabrics created for the rich . . . of more physical than spiritual value." After ten years at Nice, spent without interruption in making paintings as sensuously delightful as he could, he concluded "one may demand from painting a more profound emotion, and one which touches the spirit as well as the senses."[18] Looking to the end of the story

we can see that he was demanding nothing less than the independent, abstract recreation of ideal conditions of existence—states of visible perfection from which the least possibility of physical frustration was eliminated.

At first sight the things that Matisse was excluding from painting—the "moments of nervous excitement," the troubling subjects, and the forced expression—seem more vital than what remains. At some points in his development, the meaning he drew from the world and the meaning he gave to it were willfully, almost artificially restricted. Yet the satisfaction he demanded was so extreme that it amounted to changing the role of painting. He made painting fulfill requirements so exigent that when the demands were met at last, at the behest of the imperious old man in bed, the effect was to alter the place that painting takes in life: to alter our use for it, as cubism, for example, never did. The achievement of this change in the visual art, without forfeiting its previous luminous substance, was due to Matisse's absorption in his dream. At the present moment, thanks to Matisse, the potential of painting is far more striking than its limits.

Matisse's discovery confronted him with a difficult issue. "A work of art," he wrote, "must carry in itself its complete significance and impose it on the beholder even before he can identify the subject matter." Yet the luminous substance of nineteenth-century painting, which depended on identifiable sensations, had a special and indispensable meaning to him. Twenty years earlier, the avant-garde had faced the crisis of impressionism; the painters of the 1900's confronted the crisis of representation. But Matisse met them both together. His standpoint was necessarily more complex and apparently less decisive than those of his younger contemporaries. The formula that he arrived at had an element of equivocation: "The painter," he wrote, "must sincerely believe that he has painted only what he has seen."[17] He sometimes faltered when the belief was patently at variance with the facts. Fortunately Matisse (as he said) did not work with theory. His basic attitude was as purposeful and as single-minded as anybody's. But he was traveling in a direction opposite to virtually all the other painters of his time.

In the end, when the developments of the first half of the twentieth century were complete, it was apparent that while for his contemporaries representation of one kind or another and the basic reference to form had outlasted the luminous substance of painting, with Matisse the reverse had happened. Light had outlasted representation. In considering the apparent inconsistencies of Matisse's development, we have to bear in mind this solitary, epoch-making destination. No one else was traveling the same way. Matisse developed a self-protective, conservative attitude. He had something very personal to protect—a quality that for decades together remained inseparable from conventions of figuration that the rest of the avant-garde had finished with.

Matisse was guarding for painting a quality that was specifically visual, and sculpture came to have for him a double function. In the first decade of the century he often used sculpture to draw off the formal solidity of art into its appropriate medium, so as to leave behind in painting the strictly visual residue, flat and still. Form and formal metamorphosis were canalized into sculpture and preserved there, in case they were needed, as they eventually were. There was a streak of economy in Matisse; however lavish his purpose, nothing was wasted. In later years caution often dictated that each day's work on a picture should be photographed, lest it should be lost and irretrievable. Nothing was lost in sculpture; every stage between the realism of 1900 and the serene architectural resolution of 1930 was cast and preserved. Moreover sculpture, which offered him at intervals another fulfillment of an imaginary ideal, could also give back ideal forms to painting when they were needed again—as they were at the end of the 1920's.

Matisse's natural tendency to clarify and illuminate was already perceptible in his twenties; Gustave Moreau remarked that he was destined to simplify painting. With *Joy of Life* the process accelerated. The second version of *The Young Sailor,* 1906 (p. 26), was painted in a mood of impatience with the subtle and responsive vibrato of the first. In place of dappled mutations of green and blue, flat masses of positive color   blue, emerald, and the yellow, orange, and green that rendered flesh—were made to flower out of a plain pink background. Pink had its time of triumph in 1906: Picasso was painting pink pictures at Gosol, even Signac was working in pink. It was hardly possible to combine the empirical method with the kind of imaginative synthesis that Matisse was now in search of. His influential *Notes d'un peintre* was written in 1908 partly to demonstrate that an artist might justifiably use both in turn. His own immediate need was for a broader, more muscular form, and a visit to Italy in 1907 confirmed this direction. While Picasso set about his last pink picture, which was to change everything, *Les Demoiselles d'Avignon,* Matisse turned to monumental figure compositions of quite another kind; he took up again a wide range of primary color and evolved forms of equal simplicity and positiveness.

Matisse's synthetic method was based on an analysis of the resources of painting that was as perceptive as anything in twentieth-century art. But underneath the perceptive intelligence, there was something compulsive:

> If I put a black dot on a sheet of white paper the dot will be visible no matter how far away from it I stand—it is a clear notation; but beside this dot I place another one, and then a third. Already there is confusion. . . .

He had an acute sensitivity to the slightest hint of the disquieting confusion that threatened a picture; with every additional brushmark the threat grew closer. The only escape from it was through boldness:

> . . . In order that the first dot may maintain its value I must enlarge it as I continue putting other marks on the paper. If upon a white canvas I jot down sensations of blue, of green, of red—every new brushstroke diminishes the importance of the preceding ones. Suppose I set out to paint an interior: I have before me a cupboard; it gives me a sensation of bright red—and I put down a red that satisfies me; immediately a relation is established between this red and the white of the canvas. If I put a green near the red, if I paint in a yellow floor, there must still be between this green, this yellow, and the white of the canvas a relation that will be satisfactory to me. . . . The relation between tones must be so established that they will sustain one another.[17]

There was evidently an equal danger of disturbing conflicts between colors. It required safeguards that were as arbitrary and as drastic: "I am forced to transpose until eventually my picture may seem completely changed when, after successive modifications, the red has succeeded the green as the dominant color."[17] No more extreme reversal could be imagined. Yet Matisse made such changes freely. They were an earnest of the independence and freedom of painting.

> . . . As each element is only one of the combined forces (as in an orchestration), the whole can be changed in appearance and the feeling sought can remain the same. A black could very well replace a blue, since the expression really derives from the relationship between colors. One is not tied to a blue, green, or red if their tones can be interchanged or replaced as the feeling demands. You can also change the relationship by modifying the quantity of the elements without

Woman with Hat. (1905). Oil on canvas, 32 x 23¾". Collection Mr. and Mrs. Walter A. Haas, San Francisco

changing their nature. That is to say, the painting will still be based on a blue, a yellow, and a green, but in different proportions.[28]

There was something incongruous in Matisse's explanations of the liberties he took with representation. The younger artists were claiming much greater freedom and the leadership of the avant-garde was passing to them. Yet Matisse's almost hypochondriac sensitivity to any disorder in painting was perhaps the most progressive insight of its time. In his analysis of precisely what confusion ensues when a second and a third dot are added to the first, he was setting a new standard of intrinsic purity. Both his analysis and his example affected the whole subsequent climate of painting. The dependence of painters like Kandinsky on the visual richness of fauvism is clear enough, but Matisse's compulsive purism was of even greater significance in the years that followed.

The standard of purity he set was a high one. It demanded "Order, above all in color. Put three or four touches of color, which you have understood, upon the canvas; add another if you can—if you can't, set this canvas aside and begin again."[2] His *Notes d'un peintre* was published in many countries; his admirers organized a school in which for a year or two he taught regularly. But, however influential and articulate, Matisse remained deeply aware of the difficulty of the issue that he himself was facing. "Painting," he wrote, "is always very hard for me—always this struggle—is it natural? Yes, but why have so much of it? It is so sweet when it comes naturally."[5] When he was painting pictures like *The Red Studio*, 1911 (p. 32), he wrote, significantly, "This all or nothing is very exhausting."[4] Matisse's economy of means was not merely a matter of choice: often he felt it the only way open to him. "When difficulties held up my work, I said to myself: 'I have colors and a canvas, and I must express myself with purity even if I do it in the briefest manner by putting down four or five spots of color or by drawing four or five lines that give plastic expression.'"[1]

Nevertheless some circumstances were more favorable than others. Morocco, for example, notably reduced the gap between the reality and the dream. There was something of Matisse's ideal in the light and the style of the place, and his brush always moved more freely there. His explanation is interesting: "These visits to Morocco helped me to make a necessary transition, and to gain a closer contact with nature than would the practice of any theory such as fauvism had become, lively but somewhat limited."[10] It seems that a place, and especially a southern place, could do for him what his system and his style had been doing. It provided him with what he sought from painting—the satisfactions of a desirable state of being. The move to Nice in 1918 had an analogous effect. The light and the milieu removed the need for his previous style; it was ten years before he evolved another. The confidence in an ideally free and sumptuous world that he gained from his first short visit to North Africa, in 1906, enabled him after his return to paint one of his masterpieces, *The Blue Nude*, 1907 (p. 27). The figure, freely realized in blue planes, echoed Cézanne, like much of French painting toward the end of 1907; behind it appeared the pink and green scene of fauvism. The two were unexpectedly yet quite congruously united in memory of Biskra.

Matisse achieved his boldest synthesis of a pictorial world in decorations. The sketch of *Music*, 1907 (p. 28), *Bathers with a Turtle*, 1908 (p. 27), and the first *Dance*, 1909 (p. 29), were successive stages toward his object. He was working systematically toward the simplest yet largest and most exacting adjustment of color and form that he had ever achieved. "I shall get it," he wrote as he started on the *Dance*, "by the simplest, by the minimum of means, which are the most apt for a painter to express his inner vision."[9] The danger of disquieting confusion was to be banished finally; he ordained it like a monarch: "We are moving toward serenity by simplification of ideas and means. Our only object is wholeness. We must learn, perhaps relearn, to express ourselves by means of line. Plastic art will inspire the most direct emotion possible by the simplest means . . . three colors for a big panel of the *Dance*; blue for the sky, pink for the bodies, green for the hill."[11] As he worked the effect was intensified progressively. Later he described the result:

> My picture, *Music*, was composed of a fine blue for the sky, the bluest of blues. The surface was colored to saturation, to the point where blue, the idea of absolute blue, was conclusively present. A light green for the earth and a vibrant vermilion for the bodies. With these three colors I had my harmony of light, and also purity of tone. Notice that the color was proportionate to the form. Form was modified according to the reaction of neighboring colors. The expression came from the colored surface, which struck the spectator as a whole."[27]

The progressive process of adjustment was guided simply by the artist's reactions to what he had done. Writing about Matisse, Apollinaire concluded: "We should observe ourselves with as much curiosity as when we study a tree." Matisse probably suggested the idea; he certainly exemplified it. "My reaction at each stage," he said, "is as important as the subject . . . it is a continuous process until the moment when my work is in harmony with me. At each stage, I reach a balance, a conclusion. The next time I return to the work, if I discover a weakness in the unity, I find my way back into the picture by means of the weakness—I return through the breach—and I conceive the whole afresh. Thus the whole thing comes alive again." [28]

Matisse, in fact, grasped as early and as clearly as anyone the essential attitude of twentieth-century painting. The same self-regarding habit that had given him confidence in his direction was applied to the actual process of painting. His point of departure remained his subject, either a visible subject descended from impressionism or an arcadian one imagined on the neo-classical pattern. His method was to watch his reaction, and his reaction to the reaction, and so on, until the cumulative process gathered a momentum of its own that became irresistible. "I am simply conscious," he wrote, "of the forces I am using, and I am driven on by an idea that I really grasp only as it grows with the picture." [20] He understood an essential irrationality: "Truth and reality in art begin at the point where the artist ceases to understand what he is doing and capable of doing—yet feels in himself a force that becomes steadily stronger and more concentrated." [16] The traditional starting point might be so modified that it is lost, and replaced by a form as elemental and primitive as the color that filled it, as it was in the final state of *Music,* 1910. The result was thus hardly less disconcerting than the work of painters whose invention was centered directly on form from the first. Even so, the fact remains that Matisse's very radical purpose was in one respect conservative: he needed to retain the post-impressionist starting point, and indeed to return to it over and over again, until he had assured himself from every possible angle that he had preserved the luminous substance that he required from it.

The innovation that placed the painter and his intuitive reactions in the center of the stage was nonetheless a profound one. Even analytical cubism retained the traditional extroversion of painting: basically it was an analysis of post-impressionism, developing the discontinuities and jettisoning the color, but still outward-looking and founded on a common experience. Matisse's alternative to the extroversion was a systematic and deliberate self-engrossment. Many painters were more subjective and more inventive. He was distinguished by a certain objectivity, but what he was realistic about was himself and the way he filled the role of painter. Indeed, his view was extraordinarily acute and it yielded new information about the nature of an artistic process. Matisse discerned a method, which has now become the method of virtually all painting. Deliberately basing painting on reactions to painting, he was setting in motion the modern feed-back—the closed circuit within which the painter's intuition operates, continually intensifying qualities that are inherent. Whoever feels the radiance of Matisse's last works is experiencing the intensity that came from isolating what was intrinsic not only to a personality but to a whole tradition, and the communally conditioned reflex that it depends on.

There is hardly a greater originality in twentieth-century painting than this sedate, almost comfortable talent for self-regard. It grew on him, and it held obvious limitations, from which he did not always escape. But Matisse's standpoint, which was so close to narcissism, had a real sublimity. He was aware that the painter who is everything to himself has reason for modesty as well as pride. The reaction that he studies is not his alone; the conditioning of the reflex was not due to him. "The arts have a development that comes not only from the individual but also from a whole acquired force, the civilization that precedes us. One cannot do just anything. A talented artist cannot do whatever he pleases. If he only used his gifts, he would not exist. We are not the masters of what we produce. It is imposed on us." [28]

The inherent light in the conjunction of colors possessed a special magic for him. When he had arrived at the three colors that gave him his "harmony of light," it seemed to him that an actual radiance was generated. As a student he would put his still life in the center of the studio and call the attention of his companions to it: "Look how it lights up the room!" [7] A sour rejoinder is recorded; one of the students said that if light was the object he would rather have an oil lamp, and the future was apparently on his side. The decades that followed had no use for the idea of painting as a source of light; Matisse alone cherished it. At a certain moment in the evening, as the daylight was fading, *Dance* "suddenly seemed to vibrate and quiver." He asked Edward Steichen to come and look (when his painting puzzled him he always sent for a friend). [3] Steichen told him that the warmer illumination of evening brought the light red and the darker blue closer together in tone and set up a complementary reflex in the eye, an explanation that was certainly incorrect; in fact the reverse should have happened. In all probability the spasmodic vibration of color, which is felt when the level of illumination sinks near to the threshold of color discrimination, merely encouraged the private magic of inherent light.

It was not only painting that was luminous; his drawings shared the virtue. "They generate light; seen in a dim or indirect illumination they contain not only quality and sensitivity but also light and

variations in tone which correspond to color."[20] Matisse thought of his pictures as actually emitting a beneficent radiation; they were extensions of himself, and his excellent opinion of himself extended to them. More than once, when people who were ill looked to him to nurse them, he left a picture with them instead and went off to paint.[9]

Only his art and himself were entirely real to him. As the huge decorations came to fill his studio, more and more of the rest of existence was excluded. Painting was not only a source of painting; it became a part of his subject and soon he was representing a private world in which his own pictures shone like windows, a world that was often sufficiently peopled with his sculptures. For the rest of his life the interiors that he painted were seen as settings for his pictures that shone out as nothing else, and without the slightest incongruity. The virtue of the process was regarded as self-evident. What could art rely on more surely than on art? What could form a more proper study than oneself?

Other painters, almost without exception, were developing the structures of painting. Matisse, at first almost alone, devoted himself to the intuition that the color was real in itself. Solidity was the province of the sculptor. The structure of painting could be rudimentary; the more elemental it was, the better. The primitive had a special value to him. He is said to have introduced Picasso to Negro sculpture. He was in search of a childlike simplicity of definition. The systematic equivalence, which he had found and taught, between the colors of nature and the independent yet analogous systems of color in painting was now too complex for him. He needed not colors but color—a simple and single equivalent, hardly more than a single color. Often the chosen color was red; when he described this color method, the hue that came first was always red. His own impressive beard and hair were sandy-red. The color was seen as a continuous medium flooding everything. In *The Red Studio*, the space and its furniture are submerged in it. It is the substance of their existence; there are only the traces of yellow edges to show the immaterial frontier where separate objects once existed. The identity of things is soaked out of them—all except Matisse's own pictures. They remain themselves, simple and lovely, situated at last in their own appropriate world.

Matisse had discovered for color its deepest meaning. Color was seen as all-embracing; it resided in the nature of existence. He had discovered its capacity to make visible an ideal unlimited state of

Still Life with Eggplants. (1911). Oil on canvas, 45 x 36″. Collection Mrs. Bertram Smith, New York

being. In one or two pictures of a few months earlier the color that immersed the separateness of things was blue. In *Conversation*, 1909, which is now in Moscow, a strange emotional tension was reconciled in the calm medium of the color. Another of these interiors in which color attained this quality of universality reverted to his old subject of *la desserte*. It began as a blue picture, *La Desserte— Harmonie bleue*, with the pattern of a floral fabric covering both the table and the wall behind it, but before the picture was delivered Matisse repainted it a uniform and continuous red: the subject of laying a table, which once had been presented in steep recession with the greatest natural richness, was now embedded in a single vertical surface—inlaid in the patterned richness of the pictorial surface.

Patterns in themselves became a part of the all-pervading medium. They grew out of color. Spreading everywhere, they were the sign of its continuous, steady presence. In the famous picture of *The Painter's Family*, 1911, in Moscow, the patterns pressed round the figures, embedding them in an ever-present substance. The existence of things, even the air of obedient domesticity, was distributed evenly all over the canvas. It was indeed, as Matisse wrote, a matter of "all or nothing"; the ideal pictorial wholeness eliminated the separateness of everything.

The patterns in these pictures were inscribed as if on the surface of the canvas. They were not merely areas of illusionistic speckling and stippling like the wallpapers of the intimists. They were painted directly, as if naively, in the way cheap Mediterranean pots are painted. The proliferating patterns developed on every level. There were representations of patterns in the post-impressionist manner and patterns in the picture surface as well. Sometimes one merged imperceptibly into the other, but the pattern was all-embracing and legible. It represented at the same time an inherent property of color and a recognizable quotation. Matisse's transcriptions of the popular decorative imagery of the cultures that border on the Mediterranean played an essential and original part in his creation of an ideal pictorial milieu. They anticipated quite a different kind of painting—more closely than the popular borrowings of cubism, because they are more passive, more infatuated.

The patterns are only one of Matisse's means of making visible and pressing an inherent quality of color. They make it, in his phrase, "conclusively present." The conclusive presence of color in *The Red Studio* turns the room that is represented into something larger. The scene takes on the elemental simplicity of some basic natural situation. The spreading color envelops us; we share a common reality with the picture. Matisse wrote: "I express the space and the things that are there as naturally as if I had before me only the sun and the sky, that is, the simplest thing in the world. . . . I think only of rendering my sensations."[16] This was the culmination of the self-identification he had studied from the beginning. In pictures like *The Red Studio* we become aware of the reality of the relationship of which Matisse often spoke toward the end of his life. He explained, for example, that study allowed him "to absorb the subject of my contemplation and to identify myself with it. . . ."[6] He spoke of a painter's need for whatever "will let him become one with nature—identify himself with her, by entering into the things . . . that arouse his feelings."[22] The identification with color gave these pictures a meaning that transcends their domestic subjects. It is significant that the subjects should be domestic, for conditions of living concerned Matisse deeply, but the way in which the subject is transcended is quite outside the specific reference of European painting. In 1910 Matisse had just been to see a great exhibition of Islamic art at Munich. He said that "the Persian miniatures showed me the possibility of my sensations. That art had devices to suggest a greater space, a really plastic space. It helped me to get away from intimate painting."[11] Yet he was always clear that it was his own sensations that chiefly concerned him. His interest in everything else was strictly limited. Years later, when he was considering visiting a great exhibition of Chinese art he suddenly realized that he did not wish to: "*Je ne m'intéresse qu'à moi.*" He confessed it "with a curious and almost disarming mixture of shame and pride."[8]

The supremacy that color attained in these pictures was quite new and unparalleled. It was no longer put to any particular descriptive or expressive purpose; it was simply itself—the homogeneous, primary substance. Can anyone forget when he became aware of *The Blue Window*? In a moment one knew the simplest and most radiant idea in the whole of art—the idea that the shapes of things are immaterial except as fantastic vessels—a dish, a vase, a chalice, a bunch of balloons—to contain a bright substance of the world.

The blue fills them. They are gently inflated and rounded by the pressure. In *The Blue Window*, 1911 (p. 30), the common color presses outward with a regular, persistent pulse; the descriptive green that preceded it remains visible between the brushstrokes, but the blue has come to stand for all color, all but its precious antithesis, the ochre. In another group of pictures like *Goldfish and Sculpture*, 1911 (p. 33), and *Flowers and Ceramic Plate*, 1911 (p. 33), the hues make room for one another; they blossom together outward from the center, hardly touching. But the meaning—the sense of an equitable and serene private world made visible—re-

mains the same. These still lifes painted between the two Moroccan journeys have an incomparable air of ease; all seems well in Matisse's world. His style was already altering and soon it had changed completely. The engrossment with bright color for its own sake, which had seemed the mainspring of his work, was laid aside, as if in store, for twenty years. Matisse turned abruptly to the kind of pictorial structure that was occupying his contemporaries; the relationship with cubism, in particular, is often noticed, and sometimes misunderstood. The power to range widely and freely among the styles of his time was far from reducing what was specifically personal in his work. The constructive strength and the depth of tone, and underlying them the sense of an extraordinary control and discipline, which all reappeared in the next few years, reflected something in his artistic personality that had hardly been seen since *Carmelina*. It is clear that his final destination could never have been reached direct from fauvism: something sharp and purposeful in his nature was missing from it.

The closer contact with nature, which the visits to Morocco had gained for him, grew closer still. The spontaneity of fauvism had, as he said, become almost a matter of doctrine; it limited him. The new styles were the means of new approaches to his subject. In the portrait of *Yvonne Landsberg*, 1914—the subject of one of the most perceptive of the miniature studies that are embodied in Alfred Barr's great book—the lines of force that were drawn out of the sitter can hardly have been unconnected with the example of the futurists. Yet the device liberated a quality of energy implicit in the poise and youth of the girl, a quality that would have been beyond the reach of any other means.

These lines were carved and scraped out of the paint; Matisse's frame of mind in these years was extraordinarily ruthless, reckless and impatient. He was intolerant of anything in his way; he deleted it irritably or scratched it away (leaving untouched perhaps only his glinting, darting emblems, a pair of scarlet and crimson fish), until sometimes almost the whole of the picture seems to be made out of half-eradicated vestiges. He compelled the picture to take on a new form—a delicate but very definite structure of analogy and interplay for which there was no precedent.

A series of pictures was devoted to his painting room on the Quai St. Michel and also to the implications of painting. In one of them (now in Paris) the theme is a very precise equivalence between a subject and a picture; the equation is achieved through a resounding chord of emerald and purple. In another (in the Phillips Collection in Washington), the correspondence is one of geometry. The roundness of a nude model drawn in fat, black elliptical contours, who is posing on a square couch, is equated with a variety of elliptical images on square panels dispersed round the room, until it finds its equivalent in a round yellow tray on a square table, with a fragile-seeming vessel in the center. The primitive circle is recovered, as round as the arch of the bridge outside. The *Gourds*, 1916 (p. 31), presents a whole chain of such analogies, passing across a zone of the characteristic color of these years, a flat, unbroken black.

There survives from the first autumn of World War I a canvas, which Matisse might hardly have thought complete, called the *Open Window, Collioure*, 1914 (p. 35); it is a view between parallel vertical strips of shutter and curtain—blue, grey, and green—into black night. The darkness is ominous, yet the four colors rest calmly together on the picture surface. The vertical formulations of these years often held a sense of tension. One of the earliest of them and the most disturbing was an iron-grey picture of a *Woman on a High Stool*, 1913-14. The image was later made to preside over the tense space of the *Piano Lesson*, 1916-17 (p. 41). The subjects convey a sense of misery and mute endurance. Only the serene resolution of the pattern holds them still.

Such pictures admitted to painting some of the disquiet that it had long been Matisse's purpose to exclude. The metaphoric style permitted a curious visionary realism, and the emotional expression was deeper than ever before. The vision grew increasingly direct and simple. In *Open Window, Collioure*, the vertical structure turned into the geometry of light; the picture tells more about the natural fall of daylight than anything that Matisse had painted for ten years. The landscapes of this time were as natural and lyrical as anything he painted. The tide of color, which had flowed and ebbed, now began to flow in his work again. Matisse had learned exactly the delicate order of shape in which the color and form of nature best agreed. It is a pattern of softly distended spheres, apparently so easily come by, yet fairly containing the green and blue of earth and sky and holding them gently together.

The strenuous phase was over. For a time he seems, in his suburb of Paris, to have imagined himself in Morocco; a beautiful fluency resulted. When he moved to Nice, the place in itself was enough to maintain his sense of well-being. Painting had merely to reflect it, and Matisse soon began to imagine a special type of subject for the purpose. The endless pantomime of harems and odalisques that the unimpeachable painter and his models performed together in the twenties has now something incongruous about it. It served a purpose to the painter; with the aid of it he recovered the conditions in which he was free to move forward. He was systematically re-

storing his faith in painting as a source of undisturbed pleasure, capable of satisfying exorbitant requirements that he had not renounced. He was evidently assuring himself of the real existence of the material on which his dream depended—flooding color, pattern that was everywhere, and the abundance of every sensual delight. Solutions that he had originally arrived at imaginatively he now studied over again, at infinite leisure, from nature. His style was sometimes more naturalistic than it had been since his days as an academic student. Occasionally, as in *Odalisque with a Tambourine*, 1926 (p. 46), his approach reminds one that he owned (as well as works by Cézanne, Gauguin, and van Gogh) a nude by Courbet. He evidently needed to recover for painting the natural reference that was missing in the deliberate stylized images of the twentieth century.

The natural effects that concerned him were reviewed a good deal more systematically than the inconsequent and spontaneous style of the pictures suggested. First the common radiance of colors was identified as a quality of reflected light, filtering into calm shuttered rooms. Then he returned to his old theme of interiors filled not only with light but with the gentle, continuous pulse of southern patterns. He proceeded to relate the robust rhythms of his model more boldly to a Moorish ogee motif. Then the purpose changed again and he traced the simple forms of flesh against a regular lattice.

Flesh, with various exotic trappings, was a continual subject in the twenties and thirties. Painting from nature, he was trying to relive an impossibly voluptuous dream. Yet the issue was crucial for an art such as his, and he had never faced it directly. As always, he was quite clear about his preoccupation:

> My models . . . are the principal theme in my work. I depend entirely on my model whom I observe at liberty, and then I decide on the pose that best suits her nature. When I take a new model I guess the appropriate pose from the abandoned attitudes of repose, and then I become the slave of that pose. I often keep these girls for years, until the interest is exhausted. [20]

He was evolving the form of dream that could be depended on to last. The flesh proved transitory, indeed incongruous, but the fantasy of delight spread to embrace everything.

> . . . The emotional interest aroused in me by them does not necessarily appear in the representation of their bodies. Often it is rather in the lines, through qualities distributed over the whole canvas or paper, forming the orchestration or archi-

tecture. But not everyone sees this. Perhaps it is sublimated voluptuousness, and that may not yet be visible to everyone.[20]

His first draft of this passage ended, "I do not insist on it." [19] (The charm of the man's writings often evaporated before they saw the light.) As usual, he knew himself well. His burst of unblushing self-indulgence contributed something indispensable. The wholeness of his pictures came more and more to possess a distributed, sublimated voluptuousness. The final achievement had a pervasive quality of sensual fulfillment that was new to his work.

During most of the 1920's the consistency remained soft and luxurious. The rediscovery of the structural order and the sharpness that he required proceeded by stages. The monumentality of *Odalisque with a Tambourine* and the *Decorative Figure*, 1927, now in Paris, was apparently suggested by his sculptures. He had to eliminate what was arbitrary and evanescent, at the risk of seeming academic. When he was painting *Grey Nude*, 1929 (p. 46), he said—the imperious tone returning: "I want today a certain formal perfection and I work by concentrating my ability on giving my painting that truth that is perhaps exterior but that at a given moment is necessary if an object is to be well carried out and well realized."[18] A little later the last version of the relief of *The Back*, c. 1929, brought him close to the clean-cut simplicity that he needed.

A further step was taken after Dr. Barnes commissioned a mural on a grand scale for his foundation. A mistake in measuring the space compelled Matisse to paint the *Dance* a second time. Possibly this served a purpose; he gained a firmer grasp than ever on a scheme that was more sweepingly and deliberately planned in areas of flat color than any picture before. He invented a technique for handling these areas on the surface of the huge painting with shapes cut out of paper, colored blue and pink in gouache. For the first time he was able to take a direct hold of the basic units of his picture, just as a sculptor takes hold of his forms. The physical control of sculpture was extended to painting, and Matisse was very aware of the analogy when he turned to working with cut paper.

The arabesque of pink against blue in *The Dream*, 1935 (p. 51), still had a naturalistic, romantic reference. Matisse seems to have realized almost immediately after it was painted that this style would not lead him to his destination. He found the direction once again in his typical self-regarding, retrospective way. He looked back in particular to fauvism:

> When the means of expression have become so refined and attenuated that their expressive power wears thin, it is time

to return to the essential principles. . . . Pictures that have become refinements, subtle gradations, dissolutions without force, call for beautiful blues, reds, yellows, matter to stir the sensual depths in men. It is the starting point of fauvism: the courage to return to purity of means. [28]

Some of the pictures that followed were as freely painted as those of thirty years earlier. The apparent spontaneity of others involved a process of long adjustment, deleted time after time with white and summarily restated in bright color. The oppositions of color were bolder and flatter than they had ever been in Matisse's work. Sometimes the result was like a poetic kind of heraldry, full of subtle and sophisticated meanings. In *Lady in Blue*, 1937 (p. 49), a lady takes up a reflective pose descended from Pompeii and Ingres (like some of Picasso's sitters of the same time). Dressed in blue, she is thinking, and behind her hangs a huge blue image of head-in-hand thoughtfulness. There is an effect of rectitude and even of piety; a necklace wound round her hand is like a rosary and an emblem of repentance. Yet the mimosa-yellow nimbus that radiates from her head suggests that her natural affinity is with another image, a yellow odalisque cradling her head in her arm with sly abandon. So the picture is about attitudes and poses, and about the oppositions between a sensual yellow and a violet blue. But it is also about an all-embracing heart shape, which centers on the heart of the picture, containing yellow, red, and blue successively within one another and enclosing them all in a goblet of black—a symmetrical repeating pattern that enshrines the modish thoughtful pose and distributes its implicit voluptuousness through the picture.

Color had never been so flat and bright before, either in Matisse's painting or anyone else's. The metaphoric richness of *Lady in Blue* became characteristic of his later work. The central shape of the picture, like a heart or a vase or a flower, had a long history, stretching back through the portrait of *Yvonne Landsberg*, 1914, to the heart-shaped portrait of his daughter, *Girl with Black Cat*, 1910 (p. 28), painted twenty-seven years before. Even earlier, his teaching was full of such analogies. He would point out the likeness of the calf of a leg to a beautiful vase-form; a pelvis that fitted into the thighs suggested an amphora.[2] In the last works they served him better than ever, so that the lobed shapes his scissors outlined were not merely philodendra and polypi but the basic common shapes of everything, natural vessels for color and light.

For a time the meaning remained as sophisticated and delicate as it is in *Pineapple and Anemones*, 1940 (p. 50), but then the original impetuous reaction to colors that "contain within them . . . the power to affect the feelings" took over once again. The force of it was cumulative and astonishing. When he painted his last great series of interiors he was ready not only to sum up all his work but to add to it something of dazzling originality.

The color floods the *Large Interior in Red,* 1948 (p. 54), as it did the *Red Studio* nearly forty years earlier. But the meaning is different. The things in the room, not only the pictures on the wall but the flowers that bloom in a slight iridescent haze on the table, retain their own real quality. They remain whole, as if preserved in redness, with a new and permanent existence. Even the diagonal march of space across the floor and up into the pictures is linked with a pattern of coinciding edges, connecting tables to chair and flowers to picture, so that both are seen as natural properties of the picture's flatness and redness. We become aware that we are in the presence of the reconciliation that is only within the reach of great painters in old age. The canvas radiates it. The redness overflows and people standing in front of the picture to look are seen to have it reflected on them. They are included in it; they share in a natural condition of things and of painting.

Matisse's other mood is seen in *Interior with Egyptian Curtain,* 1948 (p. 1). The light it radiates is the vibration generated by oppositions of color. The energy that the conjunction of hues releases is more fully realized than ever. The virility is extraordinary; at last Matisse is wholly at ease with the fierce impulse. Red, green, and black together in bold shapes make the close, rich color of shadow. Outside the window, yellow, green, and black in fiery jabs make sunlight on a palm tree against the sky.

These last pictures demonstrate the nature of pictorial equivalence to the world. After meditating for more than fifty years on the pure color that the nineteenth century had placed in his hands, he had given the two basic equations of fauvism their final form. The *Interior in Red* offered intimations of elemental unity. In the *Egyptian Curtain* the interaction of color epitomized the energetic force of light. Yet the equations are so simple and self-evident that they confront one irresistibly with the element in painting that is not equated with anything. The realities are the ideal states of energy and of rest, which color creates on the picture surface.

Light, after all, could be handled directly in its own right. For a time he turned from painting to deal with it in actuality in a building, the chapel at Vence. The separable attributes of painting had finally found their appropriate forms. The reality of the picture surface remained and when he returned to the color of painting, it was as if to a natural substance. He had expanses of paper brilliantly colored to his requirements; to his delight, the doctor insisted that he wear dark glasses to go into the room where they hung. Even the streaks of the gouache were like the natural grain of a raw material. It was the basic substance of painting, the flat radiance of color. He set about it with his scissors.

When Matisse began working in cut paper he had written of drawing with scissors: "Cutting to the quick in color reminds me of the sculptor's direct carving."[21] The association was significant; he was cutting into a primal substance, the basic chromatic substance of painting, which he had extracted from impressionism and preserved intact, as if alive. The sharp edge he cut defined figure and ground, both at once, as in a carved relief. With each stroke the cutting revealed the character both of the material, the pristine substance of color, and also of an image, a subject. Whether there was an evident motif or none, there was the sense of a subject that transcended it, the radiance and movement of an ideal southern milieu. Sometimes the theme was more mobile and flowing than anything he had painted for many years; the movement was like a dance. In the greatest of the *papiers découpés,* the soaring *Souvenir of Oceania,* 1953 (p. 56), and the radiating spiral of *The Snail,* 1953, the rhythm resides simply in the action and interaction of colors. The movement springs out of a progression that begins, characteristically, with emerald. It expands in every direction, moving in great lazy leaps out to the extremes of violet and orange-red. An ideal world was completely realized and the achievement, more than any other, discovered a new reality for painting.

Late in his life, a writer tried to persuade him to pronounce against the non-figurative tendencies of young painters. He answered:

> It is always when I am in direct accord with my sensations of nature that I feel I have the right to depart from them, the better to render what I feel. Experience has always proved me right. . . . For me nature is always present. As in love, all depends on what the artist unconsciously projects on everything he sees. It is the quality of that projection, rather than the presence of a living person, that gives an artist's vision its life.[9]

ABOVE: *Dinner Table.* (1897). Oil on canvas, $39\frac{1}{2}$ x $51\frac{1}{2}$″. Stavros S. Niarchos Collection

LEFT: *Sideboard and Table.* (1899). Oil on canvas, $25\frac{7}{8}$ x $32\frac{1}{8}$″. Collection Mrs. Robert Woods Bliss, Washington, D.C.

22

BELOW LEFT: *Male Model*. (c. 1900). Oil on canvas, 39¾ x 28¾".
Collection Mr. and Mrs. Pierre Matisse, New York

BELOW RIGHT: *Standing Nude*. (1901). Oil on canvas, 31½ x 23¼".
Collection Mr. and Mrs. Gifford Phillips, Santa Monica

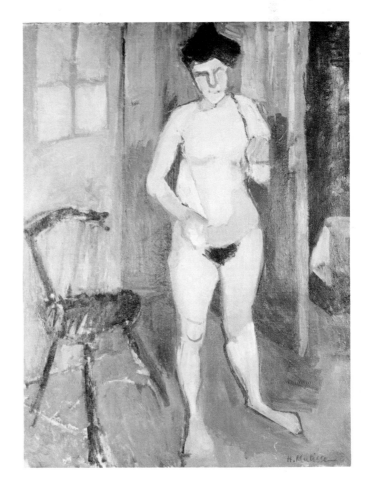

23

ABOVE: *Japanese Lady* (*Madame Matisse*). (1901). Oil on canvas, 46 x
31½″. Private collection

RIGHT: *Carmelina.* (1903). Oil on canvas, 32⅛ x 23¼″. Museum of
24   Fine Arts, Boston

ABOVE: *Luxe, Calme et Volupté* (study). (1904). Oil on canvas, 12¾ x 16″. Collection Mr. and Mrs. John Hay Whitney, New York

RIGHT: *Still Life with a Purro, I.* (1904). Oil on canvas, 23⅝ x 28¼″. The Lazarus Phillips Family Collection, Montreal

ABOVE: *Guitarist.* (1903). Oil on canvas, 21½ x 15".
Collection Mr. and Mrs. Ralph F. Colin, New York

RIGHT: *The Young Sailor, II.* 1906. Oil on canvas, 39⅜ x
31⅞". Collection Mr. and Mrs. Leigh B. Block, Chicago

ABOVE: *Bathers with a Turtle*. 1908. Oil on canvas, 5′ 10½″ x 7′ 2¾″. City Art Museum of Saint Louis, gift of Joseph Pulitzer, Jr.

RIGHT: *The Blue Nude (Souvenir of Biskra)*. (1907). Oil on canvas, 36¼ x 55⅛″. The Baltimore Museum of Art, Cone Collection

27

ABOVE LEFT: *Girl with Black Cat (Marguerite Matisse)*. 1910. Oil on canvas, 37 x 25¼". Private collection

ABOVE RIGHT: *Portrait of Pierre Matisse*. (1909). Oil on canvas, 16¼ x 13⅛". Private collection

RIGHT: *Music* (sketch). (1907). Oil on canvas, 29 x 24". The Museum of Modern Art, New York, gift of A. Conger Goodyear in honor of Alfred H. Barr, Jr.

Dance (first version). (1909). Oil on canvas, 8′ 6½″ x 12′ 9½″. The
Museum of Modern Art, New York, gift of Nelson A. Rockefeller
in honor of Alfred H. Barr, Jr.

ABOVE: *Brook with Aloes.* (1907). Oil on canvas, 28¾ x 23⅝″. D. and J. de Menil Collection

RIGHT: *The Blue Window.* (1911). Oil on canvas, 51½ x 35⅝″. The Museum of Modern Art, New York, Abby Aldrich Rockefeller Fund

ABOVE LEFT: *Marguerite Matisse with Black Velvet Ribbon.* (1916). Oil on wood, 7¼ x 6¾". Private collection

ABOVE RIGHT: *Gourds.* 1916. Oil on canvas, 25⅝ x 31⅞". The Museum of Modern Art, New York, Mrs. Simon Guggenheim Fund

31

32

OPPOSITE: *The Red Studio*. (1911). Oil on canvas, 5′ 11¼″ x 7′ 2¼″. The Museum of Modern Art, New York, Mrs. Simon Guggenheim Fund

BELOW LEFT: *Flowers and Ceramic Plate*. (1911). Oil on canvas, 36¾ x 32½″. Städtische Galerie, Frankfurt am Main

BELOW RIGHT: *Goldfish and Sculpture*. (1911). Oil on canvas, 46 x 39⅝″. The Museum of Modern Art, New York, gift of Mr. and Mrs. John Hay Whitney

33

ABOVE: *Oranges.* (1912). Oil on canvas, 37 x 33⅛″. Collection M. et Mme. Pablo Picasso, Mougins, France (Not in Exhibition)

RIGHT: *Open Window, Tangier.* (1913). Oil on canvas, 59½ x 37″.
34   Private collection

ABOVE: *Open Window, Collioure.* (1914). Oil on canvas, 46 x 35½″.
Private collection

RIGHT: *View of Notre Dame.* (1914). Oil on canvas, 57¾ x 37″.
Private collection

35

OPPOSITE: *The Green Robe*. 1916. Oil on canvas, 28¾ x 21½". Collection Mr. and Mrs. Pierre Matisse, New York

ABOVE LEFT: *Italian Woman*. (1915). Oil on canvas, 45¾ x 35". Collection Nelson A. Rockefeller, New York

ABOVE RIGHT: *Portrait of Madame Greta Prozor*. (1916). Oil on canvas, 57½ x 37¾". Private collection

BELOW LEFT: *Portrait of Sarah Stein.* 1916. Oil on canvas, 28⅝ x 22¼″.
San Francisco Museum of Art, gift of Mr. and Mrs. Walter A. Haas
to the Sarah and Michael Stein Memorial Collection

BELOW RIGHT: *Marguerite in a Fur Hat.* 1917. Oil on wood, 16⅛ x 13″.
Private collection

ABOVE LEFT: *Path in the Woods of Trivaux*. (1916). Oil on canvas, 36¼ x 28¾". Private collection

ABOVE RIGHT: *Tree near Trivaux Pond*. (c. 1916). Oil on canvas, 36½ x 29¼". The Trustees of The Tate Gallery, London

ABOVE LEFT: *The Rose Marble Table.* (1917). Oil on canvas, 57½ x 38¼″. The Museum of Modern Art, New York, Mrs. Simon Guggenheim Fund

ABOVE RIGHT: *The Pewter Jug.* (1916 or '17). Oil on canvas, 36¼ x 25⅝″. The Baltimore Museum of Art, Cone Collection

OPPOSITE: *Piano Lesson.* (1916 or '17). Oil on canvas, 8′ ½″ x 6′ 11¾″. The Museum of Modern Art, New York, Mrs. Simon Guggenheim Fund

Still Life with a Lemon. (1921?). Oil on canvas, $23\frac{5}{8}$ x $28\frac{3}{4}''$. Collection Mr. and Mrs. Richard Deutsch, Greenwich, Connecticut

ABOVE LEFT: *White Plumes.* (1919). Oil on canvas, 27⅝ x 23⅞″. The Gothenburg Art Gallery, Sweden

ABOVE RIGHT: *The Two Rays.* (1920). Oil on canvas, 36¼ x 28¾″. Norton Gallery and School of Art, West Palm Beach, Florida

LEFT: *Interior at Nice.* (1921). Oil on canvas, 52¾ x 35¼″. The Art Institute of Chicago, gift of Mrs. Gilbert W. Chapman

BELOW: *The Moorish Screen.* (1921-22). Oil on canvas, 36¼ x 29¼″. Philadelphia Museum of Art, bequest of Lisa Norris Elkins

OPPOSITE: *Woman with a Turban.* (1929-30). Oil on canvas, 70⅞ x 59⅞″. Private collection

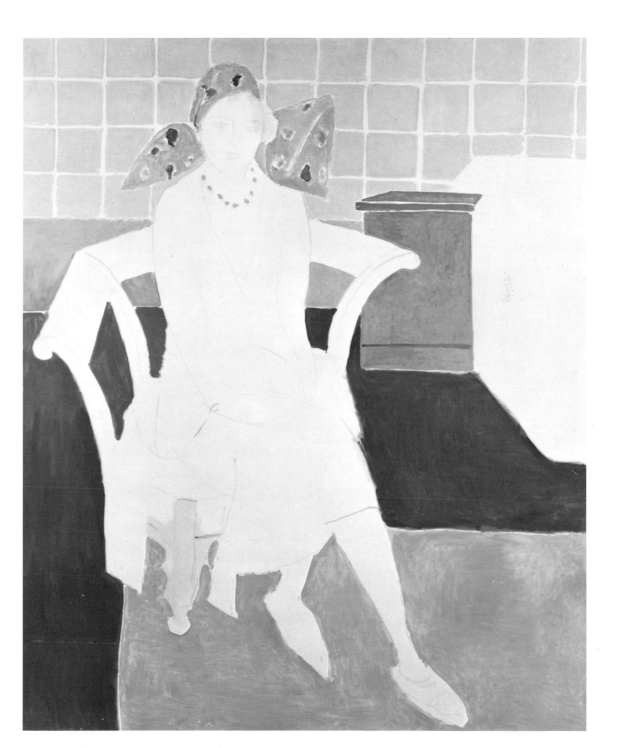

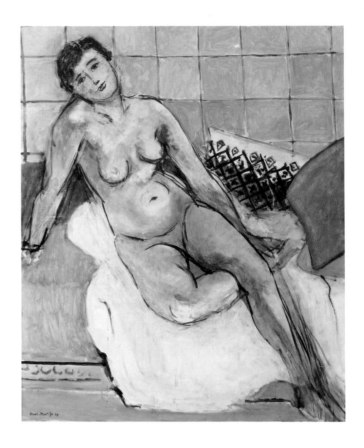

ABOVE LEFT: *Odalisque with a Tambourine*. 1926. Oil on canvas, 29 x 21⅝″. Collection Mr. and Mrs. William S. Paley, New York

ABOVE RIGHT: *Grey Nude*. 1929. Oil on canvas, 40⅛ x 32¼″. Galerie Beyeler, Basel

RIGHT: *Lemons on a Pewter Plate*. (1927). Oil on canvas, 21½ x 26″. Collection Mr. and Mrs. Nathan Cummings, Chicago

BELOW: *Reclining Nude, Back*. (1927). Oil on canvas, 26 x 36¼″. Private collection

OPPOSITE: *Odalisque with Magnolias.* (1924). Oil on canvas, 23⅝ x 31⅞″. Private collection

RIGHT: *Lady in Blue.* 1937. Oil on canvas, 36¼ x 28¾″. Collection Mrs. John Wintersteen, President of the Philadelphia Museum of Art

RIGHT: *The Magnolia Branch.* 1934. Oil on canvas, 61 x 66″. The Baltimore Museum of Art, Cone Collection

BELOW: *Pineapple and Anemones.* 1940. Oil on canvas, 29 x 36⅜″. Collection Mrs. Albert D. Lasker, New York

LEFT: *The Dream*. 1935. Oil on canvas, $31\frac{7}{8}$ x $25\frac{5}{8}$". Collection Mr. and Mrs. Pierre Matisse, New York

ABOVE: *Lemons against a Fleur-de-lis Background*. 1943. Oil on canvas, $28\frac{7}{8}$ x $24\frac{1}{4}$". The Museum of Modern Art, New York, Loula D. Lasker Bequest

51

LEFT: *Flowering Ivy.* 1941. Oil on canvas, 28½ x 36½″. Collection Mrs. Albert D. Lasker, New York

BELOW: *Dancer and Armchair, Black Background.* 1942. Oil on canvas, 19⅞ x 25⅞″. Collection Mrs. Marcel Duchamp, New York

ABOVE LEFT: *"Le silence habité des maisons."* 1947. Oil on canvas, 21⅝ x 18⅛". Private collection

ABOVE RIGHT: *Interior with Black Fern.* 1948. Oil on canvas, 45⅝ x 35". Collection Mr. and Mrs. Otto Preminger, New York

ABOVE: *Plum Blossoms, Green Background.* 1948. Oil on canvas, 45¾ x 35″. Collection Mrs. Albert D. Lasker, New York

RIGHT: *Large Interior in Red.* 1948. Oil on canvas, 57½ x 38⅜″. Musée National d'Art Moderne, Paris

REFERENCES

Quotations are drawn from the following sources. A date in parentheses shows the year of a particular quotation different from the year of publication.

1. APOLLINAIRE, GUILLAUME. Henri Matisse. *La Phalange*, Dec. 15, 1907.

2. BARR, ALFRED H., JR. Matisse: His Art and His Public. New York, The Museum of Modern Art, 1951, p. 550-552. (Remarks to the students at the Académie Matisse, recorded by Sarah Stein; 1908.)

3. BARR, *op. cit.*, p. 136. (1910.)

4. BARR, *op. cit.*, p. 152. (Postcard to Michael Stein, May 26, 1911.)

5. BARR, *op. cit.*, p. 144. (Letter to Gertrude Stein; 1912.)

6. BARR, *op. cit.*, p. 562. (Transcription of radio interviews broadcast in occupied France, sent to Pierre Matisse in New York on March 13, 1942.)

7. BUSSY, JANE SIMONE. (Unpublished memoir. Simon Bussy; 1898. Quoted by the courtesy of Professor Quentin Bell.)

8. BUSSY, *op. cit.* (1935.)

9. ESCHOLIER, RAYMOND. Matisse, ce vivant. Paris, Fayard, 1956. Also in English translation: Matisse from the Life. London, Faber & Faber, 1960.

10. ESCHOLIER, *op. cit.*, p. 104. (Tériade quoting Matisse.)

11. ESCHOLIER, *op. cit.*, p. 105. (Diehl quoting Matisse.)

12. ESCHOLIER, *op. cit.*, p. 89. (Remarks to Charles Estienne; 1909.)

13. ESCHOLIER, *op. cit.* (1947.)

14. ESCHOLIER, *op. cit.* (Message read at the opening of the museum at Le Cateau; 1952.)

15. ESCHOLIER, RAYMOND. Henri Matisse. Paris, Floury, 1937. (1936)

16. HAFTMANN, WERNER. Painting in the Twentieth Century. 2 v. London, Lund Humphries, 1960. New and expanded edition, New York, Praeger, 1965. ——Both English editions are completely revised versions of the German editions published in 1954-55 and 1957 by Prestel, Munich.

17. MATISSE, HENRI. Notes d'un peintre. *La Grande Revue*, Dec. 25, 1908.

18. MATISSE, HENRI. Interview, *L'Intransigeant*, Jan. 29, 1929. Quoted in *Formes*, v. 1, no. 1, Jan. 1930, p. 11.

19. MATISSE, HENRI. (Draft of notes in rebuttal of a proposed article by Claudinet, sent with an undated letter to Simon Bussy; 1938.)

20. MATISSE, HENRI. Notes d'un peintre sur son dessin. *Le Point*, no. 21, July 1939, p. 8-14.

21. MATISSE, HENRI. Jazz. Paris, Editions Verve, 1947.

22. MATISSE, HENRI. (Letter to Henry Clifford, Feb. 14, 1948.) In catalogue of Henri Matisse retrospective exhibition at Philadelphia Museum of Art, 1948.

23. MATISSE, HENRI. Chapelle du Rosaire des Dominicaines de Vence. Vence, 1951.

24. PUY, JEAN. Souvenirs. *Le Point*, no. 21, July 1939, p. 16-37. (1907)

25. RAYNAL, MAURICE, ARNOLD RUDLINGER, HANS BOLLIGER, JACQUES LASSAIGNE. History of Modern Painting, v. 2. Geneva, Skira, 1950.

26. SEMBAT, MARCEL. Henri Matisse. *Les Cahiers d'Aujourd'hui*, April 1913.

27. TERIADE, E. Entretien avec E. Tériade. *L'Intransigeant*, Jan. 14, 1929.

28. TERIADE, E. (Propos de Henri Matisse à Tériade.) *Minotaure*, v. 3, no. 9, Oct 15, 1936, p. 3. In article "Constance du fauvisme."

BIBLIOGRAPHY

This selective list includes, in chronological order, a small number of the most useful and currently available works that have appeared since 1951, the date of Alfred Barr's book, which remains the chief source of information on Matisse. That book contains a bibliography of earlier literature; a full list of publications since 1951 is included in the UCLA catalogue cited below.

BARR, ALFRED H., JR. Matisse: His Art and His Public. New York, The Museum of Modern Art, 1951. 591 p. ill.

GREENBERG, CLEMENT. Henri Matisse. New York, Abrams, 1953. 80 p. ill.

DIEHL, GASTON. Henri Matisse. Paris, Tisné, 1954. 167 p. ill.

DUTHUIT, GEORGES. Matisse: Période fauve. Paris, Hazan, 1956. 16 p. ill. (Petite Encyclopédie de l'Art. 2.)
Also English edition, New York, Tudor, 1956.

ESCHOLIER, RAYMOND. Matisse, ce vivant. Paris, Fayard, 1956. 286 p. ill.
Also in English translation: Matisse from the Life. London, Faber & Faber, 1960.

LIEBERMAN, WILLIAM S. Matisse: 50 Years of His Graphic Art. New York, Braziller, 1956. 150 p. ill.

FLANNER, JANET. Men and Monuments. New York, Harper, 1957. 297 p.

MATISSE, HENRI. Jazz. Munich, Piper, 1957. 51 p. ill.
Reprinted for The Museum of Modern Art, New York, 1960.

REVERDY, PIERRE & GEORGES DUTHUIT. The Last Works of Henri Matisse. New York, Harcourt Brace, 1958. 183 p. ill.
This whole work constitutes number 35/36 of Verve in the French edition.

LASSAIGNE, JACQUES. Matisse. Geneva, Skira, 1959. 138 p. ill. (The Taste of Our Time. 30.)

LEYMARIE, JEAN. Fauvism. Geneva, Skira, 1959. 165 p. ill. (The Taste of Our Time. 28.)

READ, HERBERT. A Concise History of Modern Painting. New York, Praeger, 1959. 376 p. ill.

HAFTMANN, WERNER. Painting in the Twentieth Century. 2 v. London, Lund Humphries, 1960.
New and expanded edition, New York, Praeger, 1965. —Both English editions are completely revised versions of the German editions published in 1954-55 and 1957 by Prestel, Munich.

READ, HERBERT. A Concise History of Modern Sculpture. New York, Praeger, 1964. 312 p. ill.

SELZ, JEAN. Matisse. New York, Crown, 1964. 94 p. ill.

UNIVERSITY OF CALIFORNIA, LOS ANGELES. ART COUNCIL. Henri Matisse. Retrospective 1966. Texts by Jean Leymarie, Herbert Read, William S. Lieberman. Los Angeles, UCLA, 1966. 210 p. ill.
Catalogue of exhibition organized by the UCLA Art Council and the UCLA Art Galleries with the participation of The Art Institute of Chicago and the Museum of Fine Arts, Boston.

Souvenir of Oceania. 1953. Gouache and crayon on cut-and-pasted paper, 9′ 4¾″ x 9′ 4¾″. Private collection

1869 December 31 Henri Emile Benoît Matisse born at Le Cateau-Cambrésis (Nord) in the home of his grandparents. After the war the family returns to its own home at Bohain-en-Vermandois.

1880 Pupil at the *lycée* in St. Quentin.

1887 Studies law in Paris.

1889 Passes first law examinations and returns to St. Quentin to become a clerk in a law office. Attends early-morning classes in drawing from casts at the art school at St. Quentin.

1890 Given a box of oil colors by his mother while convalescing from appendicitis. His first painting, a still life, dated in June.

1891 Abandons law and becomes a student under Bouguereau at the Académie Julian in Paris.

1892 Disgusted with Bouguereau's teaching, gains unofficial admission to the studio of Gustave Moreau at the Ecole des Beaux-Arts. Rouault, Marquet, Manguin, Piot, Guérin, and Bussy are among his fellow students. Encouraged by Moreau to copy in the Louvre. Takes an apartment at 19 Quai St. Michel.

1895 Begins to paint outdoors in Paris. Supplements his allowance by copying.

1896 Four of his paintings (two of which are sold) accepted for exhibition at the Salon du Champ-de-Mars. Elected an Associate Member of the Société Nationale. Paints in Brittany.

1897 Exhibits *Dinner Table* (p. 22), which is adversely received and badly hung. Sees the impressionist paintings hung with the Caillebotte Bequest in the Luxembourg. Works in Brittany; buys a drawing by van Gogh.

1898 Marries Amélie Parayre of Toulouse. Visits London, where he studies Turner, then spends twelve months in Corsica and Toulouse.

1899 Returns to Paris and settles at 19 Quai St. Michel. Works under Cormon, who has succeeded Moreau at the Ecole des Beaux-Arts; is asked to leave the class. Attends classes with Carrière where he meets Derain. Exhibits for the last time at the Société Nationale. Purchases with his wife's dowry Cézanne's *Three Bathers* and a plaster bust by Rodin. Also acquires *Head of a Boy* by Gauguin and a second drawing by van Gogh.

1900 Financial hardship; for a living paints exhibition decorations at the Grand Palais. Studies sculpture in the evenings.

1901 Exhibits at the Salon des Indépendants, an open exhibition under the presidency of Signac. Allowance from his father ends. Meets Vlaminck, who is working with Derain.

1902 Forced by need to return with his wife and three children to Bohain during the winter and again the following winter. While the children stay with relatives, Mme. Matisse opens a millinery shop in Paris.

1903 Founding of the Salon d'Automne, where Matisse and his associates exhibit.

1904 First one-man exhibition at the gallery of Ambroise Vollard, Paris. Spends the summer at St. Tropez, where Signac has a villa.

1905 *Luxe, Calme et Volupté* (see study, p. 25) exhibited at the Indépendants and bought by Signac. Spends the summer at Collioure with Derain. Matisse and his group, later called *les fauves,* cause a sensation at the Salon d'Automne. The Stein family begins to buy his work. Takes a studio in the Couvent des Oiseaux, Rue de Sèvres.

1906 *Joy of Life* (p. 9) (Barnes Foundation) exhibited at the Indépendants and bought by Leo Stein. One-man exhibition at the Galerie Druet. Visit to Biskra in Algeria. Summer at Collioure. Exhibits at the Salon d'Automne. Claribel and Etta Cone of Baltimore begin to collect his pictures.

1907 Exhibits *The Blue Nude* (p. 27) at the Indépendants. Goes to Italy, visiting Padua, Florence, Arezzo, and Siena. Exhibits *Music* (sketch) (p. 28) and the first version of *La Luxe* (Musée

National d'Art Moderne) at the Salon d'Automne. Exchanges paintings with Picasso, who is working on *Les Demoiselles d'Avignon*. Guillaume Apollinaire publishes an article on Matisse, recording many of his remarks. Admirers organize a school at which he teaches in the Rue de Sèvres.

1908 Moves to rooms in the Hôtel Biron, 33 Boulevard des Invalides, where his studio and school are also established. Visits Germany. Sergei I. Shchukin, a Moscow merchant, begins to collect his pictures. Edward Steichen arranges an exhibition of his drawings at Alfred Stieglitz's gallery, 291 Fifth Avenue. *Notes d'un peintre* published in *La Grande Revue*. Visits Berlin, where an exhibition is arranged that proves to be a failure.

1909 Moves to a house at Issy-les-Moulineaux, southwest of Paris, where he buys a studio. Shchukin commissions two large decorations, *Dance* and *Music* (see pp. 28-29). First version of the relief *The Back*. Summer at Cavalière, near St. Tropez. First contract with the dealer Bernheim-Jeune.

1910 Large exhibition at Bernheim-Jeune. Travels to Munich to see the exhibition of Islamic art. *Dance* and *Music* exhibited at the Salon d'Automne. Visit to Spain.

1911 Paints in Seville, Issy, and Collioure. Visits Moscow to see where his decorations are to hang. Studies Russian icons. Visits Tangier in Morocco to paint.

1912 Returns to Issy in spring. First exhibition of Matisse's sculpture arranged by Alfred Stieglitz in New York. C. T. Lund and Johannes Rump in Denmark and Ivan A. Morosov in Moscow begin to collect his pictures. Second stay in Morocco.

1913 Returns from Morocco in spring. Exhibition at Bernheim-Jeune. Participates in the Armory Show in New York. Paints at Issy; takes a studio in Paris at 19 Quai St. Michel. Exhibition of Moroccan paintings and sculptures at Bernheim-Jeune.

1914 Works at Issy. Rejected for military service. At Collioure in the autumn.

1915 Exhibition at Montross Gallery, New York. Paints at Quai St. Michel and Issy. The Italian model Lorette begins to pose for him. Visits Arcachon near Bordeaux.

1916 Paints interiors and monumental compositions at Quai St. Michel and Issy. First winter at Nice, staying at the Hôtel Beau-Rivage.

1917 Summer at Issy; autumn in Paris. At Nice from December, visiting Renoir at Cagnes.

1918 Moves to an apartment on the Boulevard des Anglais at Nice, then leases the Villa des Alliés. In Paris and Cherbourg during the summer. Autumn at Nice, taking rooms in the Hôtel de la Méditerranée and visiting Bonnard at Antibes.

1919 Exhibition at Bernheim-Jeune. Summer at Issy.

1920 Production of the ballet *Le Chant du Rossignol* by Diaghilev. Visits London with the ballet. Stays at Etretat in Normandy. Exhibition at Bernheim-Jeune of works of 1919-20.

1921 At Etretat in the summer, returning to Nice in the autumn. Moves to an apartment on the Place Charles-Félix. The Luxembourg acquires a painting. The Art Institute of Chicago buys *Woman at the Window*.

1922 From now on divides each year between Nice and Paris. The Detroit Institute of Arts acquires *The Window*.

1923 Shchukin and Morosov collections with fifty of his works combined in Museum of Modern Western Art, Moscow.

1924 Exhibition at Brummer Galleries, New York.

1925 Visit to Italy. Made a Chevalier of the Legion of Honor. Completes *Seated Nude*, his first sculpture in ten years.

1927 Awarded first prize at the Carnegie International Exhibition at Pittsburgh.

1929 Gives more time to sculpture and prints. Works on final version of *The Back*.

1930 Visits Tahiti. Serves on the jury of the Carnegie International. Visits the Barnes Foundation at Merion and Miss Etta Cone at Baltimore. Commissioned by Albert Skira to illustrate Mallarmé's poems.

1931 Accepts Dr. Barnes's commission to paint murals for the hall of his foundation and rents an empty film studio at Nice for the purpose. Large retrospective exhibition at the Galerie Georges Petit, Paris. First one-man show of a European at The Museum of Modern Art, New York, devoted to Matisse.

1932 First version of the Barnes mural completed. The measurements of the wall having been wrongly noted, begins on an entirely new version of the correct size. Mme. Lydia Delectorskaya, later his secretary and housekeeper, acts as his assistant and model. Publication of *Poésies de Stéphane Mallarmé*.

1933 Visits Merion to install the second version of the mural in the Barnes Foundation. Afterwards takes a holiday near Venice and visits Padua.

1935 Makes a design for Beauvais tapestry. Paints many compositions of the nude. Contract with the dealer Paul Rosenberg. Etchings of subjects from the Odyssey for Joyce's *Ulysses*.

1936 Exhibition of recent paintings at the Paris gallery of Paul Rosenberg. Gives Cézanne's *Three Bathers* to the Musée d'Art Moderne de la Ville de Paris. First version of the *Dance* (p. 29) shown at New York gallery of Pierre Matisse.

1937 Commissioned by Ballets Russes de Monte Carlo to design scenery and costumes for *Rouge et Noir*.

1938 Overmantel for the New York living room of Nelson Rockefeller. Paintings of models in interiors with plants. First independent *papier découpé*, a medium he has used in the preliminary work for his decorations. Moves to the former Hôtel Regina in Cimiez, a suburb behind Nice.

1939 First performances of *Rouge et Noir*. Works in the Hôtel Lutetia in Paris during the summer. Leaves Paris after the declaration of war, visiting Geneva to see the paintings from the Prado and returning to Nice in October.

1940 Spring in Paris at 132 Boulevard Montparnasse. In May leaves for Bordeaux, later staying at Ciboure near St. Jean de Luz. Decides to remain in France. Returns to Nice by Carcassonne and Marseilles. Legal separation from Mme. Matisse.

1941 Serious illness, requiring two operations in hospital at Lyons. Returns to Nice in May. From that time on often paints and draws in bed. Begins to plan the book *Florilège des Amours de Ronsard* with Skira.

1942 Exchanges paintings with Picasso. Gives two interviews over the radio of occupied France.

1943 Air raid at Cimiez. Moves inland to Vence, taking the villa Le Rêve.

1944 Commissioned to paint decorations for Señor Enchorrena. Picasso arranges for Matisse to be represented in Salon d'Automne in celebration of the liberation.

1945 Visits Paris. Retrospective exhibition at the Salon d'Automne in his honor.

1946 Exhibition at Nice. Appears in a documentary film, recording him at work and speaking of his pictures.

1947 Publication of *Jazz*, with his *pochoir* plates and text, which has occupied him for about three years. Elevated to Commander of the Legion of Honor. The new Musée National d'Art Moderne begins to assemble a representative group of his works.

1948 Paints series of vividly colored interiors. Designs a figure of St. Dominic for the church at Assy and begins work on the design and decoration of the chapel of the Rosary for the Dominican nuns at Vence. Works on big *papiers découpés*. Large retrospective exhibition at Philadelphia Museum of Art.

1949 Returns to the Hôtel Regina at Nice. Foundation stone of the Vence chapel laid. Recent paintings exhibited at Pierre Matisse Gallery, New York. *Papiers découpés* and other recent works exhibited at Musée National d'Art Moderne. Retrospective exhibition at Musée des Beaux-Arts, Lucerne. Cone collection bequeathed to The Baltimore Museum of Art.

1950 Exhibition at Nice and at the Maison de la Pensée Française in Paris. Publication of *Poèmes de Charles d'Orléans* with his lithographed illustrations and text.

1951 Completion and consecration of the Vence chapel. Exhibition organized by The Museum of Modern Art, New York, subsequently shown at Cleveland, Chicago, San Francisco, and Los Angeles. First paintings since 1948. Exhibitions in Tokyo, Hamburg, and Düsseldorf. Works on *papiers découpés* and large brush drawings. Inauguration of the Musée Matisse at Le Cateau.

1952 Exhibitions at Knokke-le-Zoute, Belgium, and Stockholm.

1953 Exhibitions of sculpture in London and at Curt Valentin Gallery in New York. Exhibition of the *papiers découpés* at Berggruen gallery in Paris.

1954 Loan exhibition of paintings at Paul Rosenberg Gallery, New York. Last *papier découpé:* design for Rose Window in memory of Abby Aldrich Rockefeller, Union Church of Pocantico Hills, New York. Represented in the French pavilion at the Venice Biennale.

November 3 dies at Nice.

CATALOGUE OF THE EXHIBITION

In dimensions, height precedes width. Dates in parentheses do not appear on the works. All works are illustrated.

Henri Matisse, 1950   Photograph by Robert Capa—Magnum

22. *Goldfish and Sculpture.* (1911). Oil on canvas, 46 x 39⅝". The Museum of Modern Art, New York, gift of Mr. and Mrs. John Hay Whitney. Ill. p. 33.

23. *The Red Studio.* (1911). Oil on canvas, 5' 11¼" x 7' 2¼". The Museum of Modern Art, New York, Mrs. Simon Guggenheim Fund. Ill. p. 32.

24. *Still Life with Eggplants.* (1911). Oil on canvas, 45 x 36". Collection Mrs. Bertram Smith, New York. Ill. p. 16.

25. *Open Window, Tangier.* (1913). Oil on canvas, 59½ x 37". Private collection. Ill. p. 34.

26. *Open Window, Collioure.* (1914). Oil on canvas, 46 x 35½". Private collection. Ill. p. 35.

27. *View of Notre Dame.* (1914). Oil on canvas, 57¾ x 37". Private collection. Ill. p. 35.

28. *Italian Woman.* (1915). Oil on canvas, 45¾ x 35". Collection Nelson A. Rockefeller, New York. Ill. p. 37.

29. *Gourds.* 1916. Oil on canvas, 25⅝ x 31⅞". The Museum of Modern Art, New York, Mrs. Simon Guggenheim Fund. Ill. p. 31.

30. *The Green Robe.* Lorette sur Fond noir. 1916. Oil on canvas, 28¾ x 21½". Collection Mr. and Mrs. Pierre Matisse, New York. Ill. p. 36.

31. *Marguerite Matisse with Black Velvet Ribbon.* (1916). Oil on wood, 7¼ x 6¾". Private collection. Ill. p. 31.

32. *Path in the Woods of Trivaux.* Le Coup de Soleil. (1916). Oil on canvas, 36¼ x 28¾". Private collection. Ill. p. 39.

33. *Portrait of Madame Greta Prozor.* (1916). Oil on canvas, 57½ x 37¾". Private collection. Ill. p. 37.

34. *Portrait of Sarah Stein.* 1916. Oil on canvas, 28⅝ x 22¼". San Francisco Museum of Art, gift of Mr. and Mrs. Walter A. Haas to the Sarah and Michael Stein Memorial Collection. Ill. p. 38.

35. *Tree near Trivaux Pond.* (c. 1916). Oil on canvas, 36½ x 29¼". The Trustees of The Tate Gallery, London. Ill. p. 39.

36. *The Pewter Jug.* (1916 or '17). Oil on canvas, 36¼ x 25⅝". The Baltimore Museum of Art, Cone Collection. Ill. p. 40.

37. *Piano Lesson.* (1916 or '17). Oil on canvas, 8' ½" x 6' 11¾". The Museum of Modern Art, New York, Mrs. Simon Guggenheim Fund. Ill. p. 41.

38. *Marguerite in a Fur Hat.* 1917. Oil on wood, 16⅛ x 13". Private collection. Ill. p. 38.

39. *The Rose Marble Table.* (1917). Oil on canvas, 57½ x 38¼". The Museum of Modern Art, New York, Mrs. Simon Guggenheim Fund. Ill. p. 40.

40. *White Plumes.* (1919). Oil on canvas, 27⅝ x 23⅞". The Gothenburg Art Gallery, Sweden. Ill. p. 43.

41. *The Two Rays.* (1920). Oil on canvas, 36¼ x 28¾". Norton Gallery and School of Art, West Palm Beach, Florida. Ill. p. 43.

42. *Interior at Nice.* (1921). Oil on canvas, 52¾ x 35¼". The Art Institute of Chicago, gift of Mrs. Gilbert W. Chapman. Ill. p. 44.

43. *Still Life with a Lemon.* (1921?). Oil on canvas, 23⅝ x 28¾". Collection Mr. and Mrs. Richard Deutsch, Greenwich, Connecticut. Ill. p. 42.

44. *The Moorish Screen.* (1921-22). Oil on canvas, 36¼ x 29¼". Philadelphia Museum of Art, bequest of Lisa Norris Elkins. Ill. p. 44.

45. *Odalisque with Magnolias.* (1924). Oil on canvas, 23⅝ x 31⅞". Private collection. Ill. p. 48.

46. *Odalisque with a Tambourine.* 1926. Oil on canvas, 29 x 21⅝". Collection Mr. and Mrs. William S. Paley, New York. Ill. p. 46.

47. *Lemons on a Pewter Plate.* (1927). Oil on canvas, 21½ x 26". Collection Mr. and Mrs. Nathan Cummings, Chicago. Ill. p. 47.

48. *Reclining Nude, Back.* (1927). Oil on canvas, 26 x 36¼". Private collection. Ill. p. 47.

49. *Grey Nude.* 1929. Oil on canvas, 40⅛ x 32¼". Galerie Beyeler, Basel. Ill. p. 46.

50. *Woman with a Turban.* (1929-30). Oil on canvas, 70⅞ x 59⅞". Private collection. Ill. p. 45.

51. *The Magnolia Branch*. 1934. Oil on canvas, 61 x 66″. The Baltimore Museum of Art, Cone Collection. Ill. p. 50.

52. *The Dream*. 1935. Oil on canvas, $31\frac{7}{8}$ x $25\frac{5}{8}$″. Collection Mr. and Mrs. Pierre Matisse, New York. Ill. p. 51.

53. *Lady in Blue*. 1937. Oil on canvas, $36\frac{1}{4}$ x $28\frac{3}{4}$″. Collection Mrs. John Wintersteen, President of the Philadelphia Museum of Art. Ill. p. 49.

54. *Pineapple and Anemones*. 1940. Oil on canvas, 29 x $36\frac{3}{8}$″. Collection Mrs. Albert D. Lasker, New York. Ill. p. 50.

55. *Flowering Ivy*. 1941. Oil on canvas, $28\frac{1}{2}$ x $36\frac{1}{2}$″. Collection Mrs. Albert D. Lasker, New York. Ill. p. 52.

56. *Dancer and Armchair, Black Background*. 1942. Oil on canvas, $19\frac{7}{8}$ x $25\frac{7}{8}$″. Collection Mrs. Marcel Duchamp, New York. Ill. p. 52.

57. *Lemons against a Fleur-de-lis Background*. 1943. Oil on canvas, $28\frac{7}{8}$ x $24\frac{1}{4}$″. The Museum of Modern Art, New York, Loula D. Lasker Bequest. Ill. p. 51.

58. *"Le silence habité des maisons."* 1947. Oil on canvas, $21\frac{5}{8}$ x $18\frac{1}{8}$″. Private collection. Ill. p. 53.

59. *Large Interior in Red*. 1948. Oil on canvas, $57\frac{1}{2}$ x $38\frac{3}{8}$″. Musée National d'Art Moderne, Paris. Ill. p. 54.

60. *Interior with Black Fern*. 1948. Oil on canvas, $45\frac{5}{8}$ x 35″. Collection Mr. and Mrs. Otto Preminger, New York. Ill. p. 53.

61. *Interior with Egyptian Curtain*. 1948. Oil on canvas, $45\frac{1}{2}$ x 35″. The Phillips Collection, Washington, D.C. Ill. p. 1.

62. *Plum Blossoms, Green Background*. 1948. Oil on canvas, $45\frac{3}{4}$ x 35″. Collection Mrs. Albert D. Lasker, New York. Ill. p. 54.

63. *Design for Red and Yellow Chasuble* (front). (c. 1950). Gouache on cut-and-pasted paper, $52\frac{1}{2}$ x $78\frac{1}{8}$″. The Museum of Modern Art, New York, acquired through the Lillie P. Bliss Bequest. Ill. p. 63.

64. *Souvenir of Oceania*. 1953. Gouache and crayon on cut-and-pasted paper, 9′ $4\frac{3}{4}$″ x 9′ $4\frac{3}{4}$″. Private collection. Ill. p. 56.

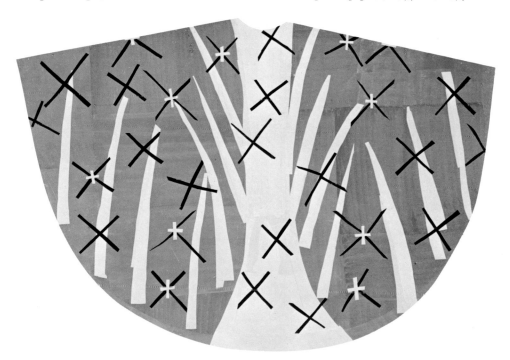

Design for Red and Yellow Chasuble (front). (c. 1950). Gouache on cut-and-pasted paper, $52\frac{1}{2}$ x $78\frac{1}{8}$″. The Museum of Modern Art, New York, acquired through the Lillie P. Bliss Bequest

63

PRINTED BY LEBANON VALLEY OFFSET COMPANY, INC., LEBANON, PENNSYLVANIA.